DOOMED
TO
FAIL

Why Government Is Incapable
of Living up to Our Hopes

PAUL SHOTTON, PHD

Published by Pierucci Publishing, P.O. Box 2074, Carbondale, Colorado 81623, USA
www.pieruccipublishing.com

Cover design by Stephanie Pierucci
Edited by Russell Womack

Hardcover ISBN: 978-1-956257-89-2
Paperback ISBN: 978-1-956257-90-8
eBook ISBN: 978-1-956257-88-5

Audiobook ISBN: 978-1-956257-87-8

Library of Congress Control Number: 2023910702

Pierucci Publishing books may be purchased in bulk at special discounts for sales promotion, corporate gifts, fund-raising, or educational purposes. Special editions can be created to specifications. For details, contact the Special Sales Department, Pierucci Publishing, PO Box 2074, Carbondale, CO 81623 or Support@Pierucci-Publishing.com or toll-free telephone at 1-855-720-1111.

DOOMED
TO
FAIL

Why Government Is Incapable
of Living up to Our Hopes

PAUL SHOTTON, PHD

PIERUCCI
PUBLISHING
ELEVATING WORLD CONSCIOUSNESS
THROUGH BOOKS

For Lynda,

Without whom this book,
and much else, would not have been possible.

TABLE OF CONTENTS

PREFACE

This book is about the nature of human societies and the things we create to help us organize our lives; things such as polities, political and economic frameworks, and the institutions that societies develop in support of good governance. The range of topics covered may seem at first sight to be overly broad and unfocused, but as I shall explain, there are important reasons why it is necessary for us to paint on a broad canvas, and why specialization in a narrower field of study is inappropriate for the nature of the matters I shall discuss.

There are those who will say that I, as a trained physicist with a PhD from the University of Oxford, and who has undertaken research at the European Centre for Nuclear Physics Research into the fundamental forces of nature and the elementary particles which make up all of matter, but who has no formal training in economics, politics, nor international relations, am unqualified to discuss the matters with which this book is concerned. We must ignore such siren voices. For one thing, they are entirely self-serving, principally being an argument for protection of those who are so qualified in the same way that the ancient craft guilds attempted to prevent competition from outsiders in order to maintain high prices for the things the craftsmen created, purely for the benefit of guild members at the expense of consumers. Credentialism is one of the banes of modern American society, persuading, as it does, many millions of young people to waste their time and money, often in the process accumulating huge amounts of student loan debt, only to gain a useless college degree which is completely unnecessary and confers upon them absolutely no advantage in the career which they will subsequently undertake.

But more important than their protectionism, the argument is fundamentally wrong for reasons I will explain. Human societies are examples of what are described as mathematically complex adaptive systems. Such systems have several important properties, including that there are deep interconnections between the various components of the system, and that they tend to obey power laws so that small uncertainties in the starting conditions lead to much-magnified differences in outputs. The deep interconnections render invalid the classic technique of Stoic philosophers of breaking down a complicated problem into its component parts, and then employing experts to solve each component before reconstituting the whole. This method will work for problems which are merely complicated, but not for problems which are mathematically complex, as are the problems I shall discuss in this book.

In recent years, the world has been undergoing simultaneous crises in four separate such systems. Countries around the world, including the United States, have been enduring crises of politics and political legitimacy with increasing polarization, tribalism, and extremism in what hitherto had been seen as rock-solid, stable polities. We have endured an ongoing global economic crisis due to the fallout from the Global Financial Crisis of 2007–2009, and the political response to it. This has been exacerbated by a global health crisis due to the coronavirus pandemic, which is only now, more than three years later, beginning to subside. And finally, we are experiencing the effects of a slow-moving crisis due to global climate change which is alternately causing droughts, floods, storms, and unseasonal weather extremes to differing degrees in many countries, inevitably with those least able to manage its consequences experiencing the most damaging effects.

Whilst each of these systems is complex, adaptive, and deeply interconnected internally, not only are there deep interconnections between components within each system, but there are also complex interactions *between systems*. This renders moot the specialized knowledge which any expert can have about any one narrow aspect of a system when that expertise is required to be factored into a means of decision making which must reflect and impact the whole set of interconnected systems.

The result of this complexity is that to make sound decisions we would need to be experts in multiple fields of study, to a degree which, practically, is impossible. This does not mean that we should completely ignore the advice of experts, nor that we should throw up our hands in despair, bury our heads in the sand, and sit, paralyzed, incapable of making any decision at all. But it does require us to have a healthy skepticism of experts who claim with great confidence that they have the correct solution. As Bertrand Russell so eloquently put it: *"The fundamental cause of trouble in the world today is that the stupid are cocksure while the intelligent are full of doubt."*

We must marshall the facts and construct our arguments accordingly, interpolating between and extrapolating from the data points we have, using reasonable assumptions and logic, to take us into the realms where we have not yet collected data. We must then test empirically to make sure that newly observed data are aligned with our theoretical model, in accordance with the scientific method. Karl Popper's philosophy of science as an open belief system in which every theory is open to scrutiny and testing, and his description of the logical asymmetry between verification and falsifiability: to verify a theory as being correct would require us to test its predictions at every point of time and space, whereas all it takes is one discordant data point to prove that a theory is false and leads to what the great Victorian biologist Thomas Huxley described as, *"The great tragedy of science is the slaying of a beautiful hypothesis by an ugly fact."*

But provided we use the data soundly, making justifiable assumptions and logic to make sensible deductions, draw sensible conclusions, make decisions and finally execute actions, we are following a method which has driven more technological and scientific progress in the last 350 years than during all of the preceding lifespan of humanity.

Of course, we may not always like where our deductions take us. I am as prone to cultural, political, and other biases as anyone else, given my upbringing and life experiences, which have helped shape my views. Sometimes I am surprised by the direction my logical deductions take and the conclusions I draw. When this happens, I am forced to change my opinions; this is the honest approach to using the scientific method. With apologies to the late author Sir Arthur Conan Doyle for the alteration I make here to the words I am reminded of which he put into the mouth of one of my childhood fictional heroes, the detective Sherlock Holmes, *"When you have eliminated the untenable, whatever remains, however unpalatable, must be the truth"*. But certain ideas follow from this; in particular:

Never let anyone tell you that you do not have the right to an opinion.

Never let anyone tell you that you should stick to your knitting.

Ultimately, the big difference between me and formally trained economists is that I don't suffer from physics-envy.

INTRODUCTION

In the period of almost 250 years since our country was founded, the American experiment in democracy has seen much turbulence, from the lows plumbed during the Civil War, to a peak in the aftermath of the Second World War when the United States displaced Britain as the global hegemon and established the Pax Americana which has governed global relations ever since. With the success of American-imposed democracy on the war's losing Axis powers, Germany and Japan, and with the collapse of the Soviet Union and the end of the Cold War, the world saw a unipolar moment which was the zenith of American economic and military power. At the time, there was real hope that over time China would adopt democracy as its political model and capitalism as its economic model. Indeed, liberal democracy and capitalism seemed set to be adopted as the preferred political and economic models around the world, leading Francis Fukuyama to write *The End of History*.

However, as the twenty-first century has unfolded, the hopes for the twin triumphs of democracy and capitalism appear to have been dashed. Whilst doubtless, there are several contributory factors, including the downsides of globalization which have negatively impacted the middle classes in developed countries, the rise of Xi Jinping as dictator in China, and a militaristic Vladimir Putin in Russia, much of the cause of the malaise may be laid at the door of the Global Financial Crisis between 2007 and 2009. In addition to demonstrating the failure of the political elite throughout the world's leading industrialized economies who were seen to have feet of clay being self-serving and increasingly taking a bigger share of the economic pie for themselves at the expense of everyone else, the crisis was also a failure of political institutions, in particular the central banks, led by the Federal Reserve Bank of the United States.

Established by an act of Congress just two days before Christmas of 1913, on a near party-line vote with Democrats in favor and Republicans largely against, in the aftermath of the Knickerbocker Trust Crisis of 1907, the Fed was charged initially with maintaining the stability of the financial system. The Fed's responsibilities were subsequently expanded to include low and stable inflation and full employment for the U.S. economy. These three elements, often described as the Fed's "dual mandate" (suggesting that their numeracy is about as good as their understanding of economics and the economy) have remained the Federal Reserve's core responsibilities, and, as will be discussed in later chapters, has been seen to fall well short on all these tasks. The Fed's mismanagement of monetary policy and its failure to supervise banks properly led to the Global Financial Crisis, and its actions in the aftermath exacerbated its effects, driving increased unemployment and subsequently a boom in financial asset prices and increased wealth disparity. The long history of the Fed is one of its cleaning-up messes of its own creation, and we would all be better off without it.

Although the path the United States has taken in recent years has led it to a bad place, the country remains both the greatest and the greatest force for good in the world. In this book, I shall explain why democracy remains the best political system and why capitalism remains the best economic system. Given the prominent role of the Federal Reserve in causing and exacerbating the Global Financial Crisis, and the centrality of the Crisis in causing the country's loss of faith in democracy and capitalism, this book will explain the Fed's role in the failures at some length, and following on from that, explain why that institution is not fit for purpose and needs fundamental reform. Although one of the principal actors, the Federal Reserve is not alone in deserving our opprobrium; there are many other things the country must address to restore itself to a good path; but they are beyond the scope of this book. Instead, I shall address those in a future work: *What Ails America?* And how to fix it.

CHAPTER ONE:

COMPLEX ADAPTIVE SYSTEMS

Although the quotation is often misattributed to the New York Yankees catcher Yogi Berra, because it's the kind of thing Berra might have said, it was actually the quantum physicist Nils Bohr who said: *"Making predictions is difficult, especially about the future."* That the future is difficult to predict should not be surprising; as the economist Frank Knight explained, not only is the future unknown, but it is unknowable.

Of course, some things in the future are knowable with a high degree of accuracy; the fact that the sun will rise tomorrow morning should not come as a surprise to anyone, nor should the timing of its rising and setting, nor the times of the vernal and autumnal equinoxes and the summer and winter solstices. These are all examples of physical phenomena which are well understood and have been since at least the time of Sir Isaac Newton, one of the greatest physicists who ever lived, and who, amongst his other great feats, developed the first theory to successfully describe celestial mechanics. Although in 1915, Newton's explanations of gravity and the motions of heavenly bodies were supplanted by Albert Einstein's theory of general relativity, for most everyday purposes, classical Newtonian mechanics is perfectly adequate to describe such physical phenomena. In terms of physical systems, it is only when we approach the very smallest scales or when we are traveling at speeds approaching that of light, which is finite, that we need to leave the realm of classical mechanics and invoke the superior explanatory power of quantum mechanics and the special and general theories of relativity.

After his financial losses in the scandal of the South Sea Bubble, Newton himself said: "*I can calculate the motion of heavenly bodies, but not the madness of people.*" That the motion of heavenly bodies is predictable whilst predicting the future in respect of human affairs does not stem from the fact that the solar system and other physical systems like it are relatively simple, whereas the nature of human society is that it forms a ***complex adaptive system***.

Wikipedia describes complex adaptive systems as "a subset of non-linear dynamical systems consisting of a dynamic network of interactions, with the behavior of the ensemble not reliably predictable according to the behavior of the components." The complexity of these systems stems from the deep interconnections between the different system components and their non-linearity. They tend to follow power laws so that small uncertainties in the starting conditions lead to much-magnified differences in outputs, rendering forecasts highly likely to be way off-beam. Their adaptive property comes about because the individual and collective behavior of the system components mutate and self-organize corresponding to change-initiating endogenous or exogenous micro-events or collections of events.

Another way of saying this is that these systems change over time, with many changes being caused by the actions of the participants within the system themselves, as well as by factors which may be regarded as outside the system. In this way, complex adaptive systems are more akin to the physical systems of quantum mechanics, which describe systems on the atomic scale, rather than those of classical mechanics, which describe the mechanics of physical systems on an everyday human scale. In the former, the elements of the system are so small that the very action of observing the system may disturb it and change its outcomes, a phenomenon described by Heisenberg's *Uncertainty Principle*. In the context of financial markets, George Soros refers to this property as "reflexivity", and at its root it is the cause of Goodhart's Law, which is the observation of the economist Charles Goodhart, that whenever policymakers discovered a correlation between two economic variables and then started to target one of the variables in an attempt to influence the other, the correlation immediately broke down.

In contrast to the physics of systems on the atomic scale, in physical systems on a human scale, which are adequately described by the laws of classical physics, there is complete independence between the system under observation and the person doing the observing. The actions of the observer don't change the system under observation.

People often refer to financial markets as being like a casino or gambling at the racetrack, but those who draw this analogy are missing a crucial distinction. When betting on a horse at the racetrack or on the turn of a card in the casino, there is complete independence between the result of the event – which horse wins the race, or which card turns up – and the betting market. Bets placed by punters will influence the odds made by bookmakers, who shorten the odds of those horses most favored to win, for example, and lengthen the odds of the other horses, but none of this action in the betting market influences the result of the race; in the end the race is won by the best horse on that day. This independence between the betting market and the event we are betting on renders systems of this kind akin to those of classical physics.

In the interactions of human societies, however, there is no such independence. The actions of one participant can and do influence the actions of other participants, as can exogenous changes to other features of the system. For example, if the price of a food item, say pork, increases due to a shortage of hogs, consumers are likely to try to avoid the effect of the price hike by substituting some other, cheaper, food item, such as chicken. Consider now a second example: If a government tries to increase its revenue by increasing a tax rate, those people subject to the increased tax are unlikely to just sit there waiting for their pockets to be picked by the IRS. Instead, they are highly likely to rearrange their affairs in such a way as to minimize their exposure to the rate increase, and as a result there is likely to be a shortfall relative to the amount of revenue the government projected it would generate by increasing the tax rate. These are examples of the adaptation process which interactions in all human societies experience.

Likewise, in financial markets, there is no independence between observer and observed. In this case, it's the buying- and selling-pressure from market participants which produces the market outcomes, as positive sentiment from buyers bids-up the price of an asset, and likewise negative sentiment from sellers pushes down the price. John Maynard Keynes gave the analogy that successful investment in the stock market is like trying to predict the winner of a beauty contest; we are not trying to pick the contestant whom we ourselves believe to be the most beautiful, but rather pick the contestant whom we think the majority of the judges will think is the most beautiful. In other words, to profit from the rising price of a stock we need to identify the stock which most other investors will buy, because it's their buying-action which will push up its price. It's this interaction between market participants and market outcomes which makes financial markets more akin to the world of quantum mechanics, and which makes financial markets adaptive.

Financial markets, political frameworks, the coronavirus pandemic, and global climate change are all examples of systems which exhibit the properties of complex adaptive systems and which are more akin, therefore to the world of quantum mechanics. They cannot be treated as though they obeyed the rules of classical mechanics with independence between observer and observed. They are not tractable by the techniques of Stoic philosophers because of the complexity and deep interconnections between the different components of the system. In fact, not only are there deep interconnections between components within each system, but components are also subject to interconnections between systems.

An example of interconnections between two different systems which we have all witnessed recently is that of the global climate crisis with the global economy. Many climate experts are calling for rapid decarbonization and withdrawal of capital from carbon-extractive industries to accelerate the transition to the use of renewable energy sources in order to lessen the impacts of climate change, despite the fact that this will have a severe impact on economic well-being, especially for poorer people. This results from higher energy prices because the necessary infrastructure to supply clean energy from renewable sources is not yet sufficiently developed. This tension between addressing a problem in the global climate system – to reduce CO_2 emissions as quickly as possible – at the expense of creating an economic problem is entirely typical of complex adaptive systems.

For all that the understanding of how each of these systems works requires extensive knowledge and expertise, the fact that the systems are interdependent renders the knowledge of experts moot since experts tend to exhibit their specialist knowledge in only a narrow field of study.

During the campaigning ahead of the referendum on whether the UK should remain in or leave the European Union, Michael Gove, a former Secretary of State for the Department of Education, amongst other government offices, famously declared: "The British people have had enough of experts!" Having witnessed the shambles which Gove and his Tory colleagues subsequently made of Brexit following the results of the vote, and the UK's more recent political and gilt market gyrations, I think we can safely say that by now the British people have had their fill of incompetents, too. But despite the fact that Gove's comment was much ridiculed at the time, there is nevertheless a grain of truth in what he was saying; namely, that experts are able to demonstrate their expertise in only a narrow field, whereas the real world is extremely complex, multi-faceted, and interconnected; a complex adaptive system.

Over time, belief in the value of expertise goes in and out of fashion. At the turn of the twentieth century, Victorian scientists such as Lord Kelvin believed that they had conquered the physical world, and that *"There is nothing new to be discovered in physics now. All that remains is more and more precise measurement."* Yet within just a few years, the scientific revolutions of Relativity Theory and Quantum Mechanics overthrew the world of classical physics. Spectacular achievements in fundamental science, medicine, biology, and technology during the twentieth century gave rise to a belief in the power of the scientific method, and that, given enough time, money and effort, all of nature's secrets could ultimately be revealed. And yet during our own time, faith in the abilities of experts in all fields has declined. Often, this has been due to personal failings on the part of the experts, some of whom were seen to have manipulated the data or cheated in other ways when publishing the eye-catching results of their analyses in an attempt to secure tenure, funding for more research, or some other sinecure. Other times it was because the experts were seen to have colored the outcomes of their research to conform to the desires of a financial sponsor or a political imperative. They were seen not to be the dispassionate seekers-after-truth that they had claimed. Instead of being disinterested and allowing the facts to do the talking, they were seen to express partisan views and have ulterior motives.

In the field of medicine, instead of following Hippocrates' dictum "first, do no harm," experts express a tendency to want to intervene to address perceived physical ailments, as though the body of knowledge collated during a few hundred years of medical practice can do more to make the human body more fit for its environment than has tens of thousands of years of evolution. Sometimes the wish to intervene may stem from a desire to experiment and increase knowledge, but other times it may be to advance the agenda of a third party; for example, a pharmaceutical company wanting to sell more drugs regardless of whether or not the drugs might have any therapeutic benefit. To be sure, there have been great advances in medical knowledge and treatments, alongside improved sanitation and nutrition, allowing a doubling of the average human lifespan during the last 150 years; but how often do we observe a medical specialist recommend treatment for some ailment, oblivious of the fact that the patient may have some other medical condition in which field the specialist has little knowledge, but for which the treatment he has just recommended is contraindicated? General holistic knowledge beats specialization for such a patient.

Expertise tends to demonstrate its value whenever the system or process under consideration is linear, non-complex and non-adaptive. In setups of this type, centralized decision making, standardization, and uniform practices make sense, too. As an example, consider the situation of a system of weights and measures. If each of us adopted our own means of measuring lengths, weights, volumes, and so on, then trade between counterparties, one of the bedrocks of wealth creation as described by Adam Smith and David Ricardo, would become much less efficient. How many of us who have international colleagues have been frustrated to receive a document nicely formatted to print on one side of standard European A4 paper, only to print it out on the quite similar, but slightly different-sized, U.S. standard letter paper, and see the text spill over onto two pages? Even more frustrating is the experience of the American visitor to the United Kingdom who plugs their hair dryer designed for standard U.S. 60 Hertz 120 Volt power into a UK socket (having bought from the airport an adapter to allow the two plain pegs of the U.S. plug to fit into the three square-pin sockets of the UK power supply) only to blow the fuse, if not the motor, of the dryer, thanks to the UK's standard 50 Hertz 240 Volt power supply. The power supplies in either country, as on the European continent, are all perfectly fine provided that you are using an appliance designed for use with that system; but international travel is made more difficult, and the cost of appliances in every country is made much higher than they would need to be if there was a global standard of power supply and appliances.

Maintenance of differing measurement standards in different countries often results in costly errors. When the Hubble space telescope was launched in 1990, astronomers were disappointed to find that the early pictures sent back to earth from the telescope were much fuzzier than they had expected. After some investigation, it was discovered that the reason lay in the fact that when the primary mirror for the telescope was ground by the Perkin Elmer corporation of Danbury, Connecticut in the USA, the manufacturer assumed that the dimensions which had been sent were in inches, still standard measures of length in the U.S., whereas in fact the specification sent by the designer had been measured in centimeters, part of the Systeme Internationale (SI) metric system common in Europe. Only after corrective optics and new instruments (akin to giving Hubble a pair of spectacles) was installed by spacewalking astronauts during a space shuttle mission in 1993 was the telescope able to transmit images of the quality and resolution originally intended.

In the early days of any new technology, it makes sense to allow a variety of different would-be standards to compete until a best practice emerges. Once the industry consolidates around a preferred standard, it makes sense, subsequently, for the entire world to adopt it. This process doesn't always work, however. It is widely regarded that in the early days of the competition between the Sony-backed Betamax format for video tapes with that of the JVC-developed VHS system, Betamax was technically superior and was actually the first-mover; but nevertheless, VHS prevailed in the subsequent format-wars of the late 1970s and early 1980s, principally because of the longer recording time its cassettes offered, the fact that a bigger library of recorded films was available in VHS, and because more hardware manufacturers supported VHS, resulting in a competition-driven lower price for VHS equipment.

Although commonly adopted standards would benefit consumers throughout the globe through the lower prices resulting from simpler manufacturing processes and more international competition, the sunk-cost fallacy often prevents this. The problem is that once the initial financial outlays have been made in installing certain equipment, there is a tendency to want to recoup value from the capital invested, even though economically that should be regarded as a sunk cost, and evaluations of future investments should be made on a forward-looking basis of what will deliver the best return in the future, regardless of what might have been spent in the past. The sunk cost fallacy is typical of the flaws of human nature; Homo *sapiens* rarely behave as the economically rational Homo *economicus* would. But once extensive infrastructure has been built, systemic inertia renders subsequent change virtually impossible. Imagine the uproar if the United Kingdom were to decide to switch to driving on the right-hand side of the road, as most of the world does, instead of on the left, to save money in the long term on the price of cars. Whilst there would be an economic benefit from such a shift, its effects would be recouped only over the long term and most people would agree that the disruption in the short term would outweigh the benefits; so, drivers in the UK and in a few other countries are stuck with driving on the left and higher vehicle prices.

So, we can see that there are some things for which the adoption of national (if not international or global) centralized standards would work best, yet there are others for which decentralized decision-making would be best. The question is how to decide which technique to adopt for which kind of problem. The answer lies in the nature of the problem. Those problems which concern situations which are neither complex (in a mathematical sense; they may still be complicated) nor adaptive lend themselves to treatment by a uniform centralized process, best informed by the expertise of people who have given thought to how best to arrange them or been trained to operate in them. In contrast, in a complex and adaptive system such as a political or economic system or a financial market, then a wisdom-of-crowds approach works best.

Piloting an airplane, for example, may be complicated, and may require many hours of training to do safely; but it is not complex. When flying on a plane, I would much rather it be piloted by an expert (ideally with another trained pilot as back-up) than according to the collective wisdom of the passengers. Likewise, designing a power grid would be best if standardized globally and left to experts.

In contrast, during the pandemic, we heard calls from officials and the medical experts to "follow the science," whilst economic policymakers are often wont to say that future policy moves are "data dependent." Given the nature of these kinds of problems, which exist within a complex space, whilst it is always a good idea to take the data, the analytical research, and the opinions of experts into consideration when forming a judgment, handing-over responsibility for making the ultimate decision to the experts is unwise because the range of their expertise is too narrow. The world of these kinds of problems is simply far too complex to allow such a method to be successful, and calls instead for a more holistic approach.

What the world has faced in recent years has been simultaneous crises in four distinct systems, each one of which is an example of a complex adaptive system. Not only are these systems complex and deeply interconnected within themselves, the four systems interact with each other, resulting in highly complex compounding behavior. That experts tend to exhibit their expertise in only a relatively narrow field explains why it was of only limited value in helping governments navigate their way through the crises.

So, what are the four systems I am referring to? First, and most obviously, we had the coronavirus pandemic for which experts were advising lockdowns, social distancing, shelter-at-home, mask-wearing, and so on, until vaccines started to become widely available.

The second system, which continues to be in crisis, is the real economy, which suffered from relatively low economic growth caused by extreme government indebtedness after the Global Financial Crisis, which indebtedness was further exacerbated by the fiscal policy response to the pandemic, as shown in the chart shown below, courtesy of the Federal Reserve Bank of St. Louis FRED database.

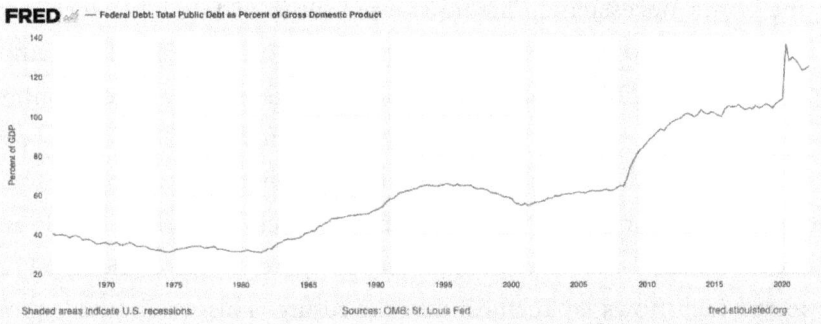

FRED — Federal Debt: Total Public Debt as Percent of Gross Domestic Product

Shaded areas indicate U.S. recessions.　　　Sources: OMB; St. Louis Fed　　　fred.stlouisfed.org

In the aftermath of the pandemic, economies were on life support in the form of excessively easy monetary policy in the form of very low or negative interest rates and quantitative easing; but the combination of loose monetary policy and excessive fiscal stimulus, coupled with supply chain shocks and changes in peoples' spending habits due to the pandemic, and further exacerbated by the war in Ukraine, led to a surge in inflation, which the central banks were initially slow to react to, arguing that the inflation was transitory and due to base-level effects. Central banks were also slow to react because of an asymmetric stance towards inflation. Having presided over a long period when both inflation and economic growth were very low, central banks were fearful that economies might tip into deflation and the risk of a depression, so they deliberately acted to allow the economy and inflation to "run hot" for a while to counteract the earlier period of inflation below the target they had set of 2%. An additional factor was that the chairman of the Board of Governors of the Federal Reserve, Jay Powell, was leaned on by President Trump to keep interest rates low to aid his reelection campaign in 2020, and then Powell's own bid for renomination after his first term as Fed Chair expired in 2021, led him to keep rates lower than was wise in order to secure his renomination by the incoming President Biden.

For all these reasons, the Fed was slow to act, and by the time they belatedly started to raise rates, the inflation genie was well-and-truly out of the bottle, necessitating the most rapid series of rate hikes seen since at least the Second World War. But having been on the drug of extremely loose monetary policy for an extended period of time, the economy became addicted, and the withdrawal of low rates led to the collapse of extremely overvalued financial markets and other markers of financial excess, including crypto, NFTs, and meme-stocks as well as bonds and equities. Initially, the instruments hit the hardest were those whose expected cash-flows lay furthest into the future. This was because those instruments have the longest duration and thus interest rate sensitivity. (Duration is a concept most commonly thought of in respect of fixed income securities, but equities also have a duration. In both instruments, duration is calculated as the weighted average time to receipt of the cash-flows generated by the security, so bonds with low coupons and equities which don't pay dividends, such as the tech stocks, have a very long duration. They are therefore particularly sensitive to changes in interest rates, and when rates rose aggressively, their prices, being the present value of the discounted expected future cash flows, fell dramatically.)

Central banks were never able to normalize rates nor withdraw quantitative easing in the aftermath of the Global Financial Crisis, and then the economic shock resulting from the coronavirus pandemic made things much worse. Note that the solutions offered by the medical experts in respect of the coronavirus, of lockdowns, social distancing, etc., made the economic crisis much worse, whilst the prescriptions of the economists to help the economy risked making the pandemic much worse. Such contradictions between remedies, confounding the advice of experts, are entirely typical of complex adaptive systems.

The third system in crisis is that of our political framework which has been undergoing a crisis of political legitimacy. The failure of the political elite to prevent the Global Financial Crisis, and policymakers' response to it, characterized as bailing out Wall Street at the expense of Main Street, is seen to have increased wealth disparity, with the wealthy benefitting from the rise in asset values driven by monetary easing, whilst young people just beginning their careers, and poorer people who do not own financial assets, losing their jobs, or having only very tenuous jobs in the gig economy.

Trickle-down economics, the idea that boosting the wealth of the elite would lead to the trickling-down of wealth to the lower rungs of the economic ladder as the rich used the liquidity offered by the Fed and their newfound wealth through higher asset prices to invest in new businesses and increased production capacity, thus creating well-paid jobs for the less wealthy, was found to be fanciful. To believe that such an indirect route to address the needs of the less well-off would be successful was always dubious, and so it proved. The failure of the elite to prevent the crisis came on top of a long period of industrial decline and job losses for the middle classes as globalization saw the offshoring of manufacturing to China and other countries offering lower labor costs. Whilst such outsourcing and offshoring made sense in the short-term from a purely economic perspective – after all, David Ricardo had explained in the early nineteenth century how trade generates wealth through his theory of comparative advantage – nevertheless, the elites failed to address the issues which it would create. The assumption was that as everyone would benefit from the lower-cost items and lower inflation which would result from sourcing cheaper labor overseas – even those who were losing their jobs to overseas competitors – then the loss of jobs for the displaced middle class was a price worth paying. Of course, this kind of economic rationale is easy to justify for those whose own jobs are not at risk. But social cohesion is as important for a polity as is economic efficiency. Had the wisdom of the elite matched their greed, they would have realized that it would be necessary to offer a helping hand to those of their compatriots who would suffer the job losses resulting from globalization. They would have had the good sense to share the economic bounty they would reap from globalization by paying more – in taxes for example – so that the displaced could be retrained in a new skill or occupation and found a place in the new economy as a valued member of the home team. But no, the selfish greed of the elite exceeded their wisdom, and as a result we have seen the social strife and increased political polarization of recent years.

We have witnessed similar polarization across liberal democracies, in Europe and the UK in particular, not just the United States. Whilst ostensibly the vote in favor of Brexit in the UK in 2016 was about taking back control from the European Union in Brussels, in reality it was about the left-behind English regions – people living in post-industrial cities such as Stoke-on-Trent and Sunderland – taking back control from an overly centralized concentration of wealth and power in London and the Southeast, and a rejection of everything that London and the European project stand for in terms of globalization, free trade and the free movement of people. Of course, impoverishing London is not going to help Stoke, but people experience wealth on a relative basis. If the gap in living standards between London and Stoke is reduced then it makes the people living in Stoke feel better, even if both sets of people are in fact poorer.

Recognizing this view of wealth, the elite would be wise not to let the gap between rich and poor become too large. Historically there have been periodic swings in wealth disparity, but the pendulum cannot swing too far in one direction before it becomes subject to violent reversals, usually literally, thanks to wars and revolutions. It would behoove the elite to prevent the pendulum from swinging too far of their own volition, to allow their privileged excess to continue for as long as possible, but as I have already commented, usually their greed and desire for further dispersion within their own class exceeds their wisdom. As a result, they risk bringing the whole privileged edifice crashing down around their heads.

Capitalism is perceived as having failed the middle classes, and democracy is perceived as having been exploited by the political elite and the well-connected – what some have referred to as "the protected class" – for their own benefit. According to surveys conducted by Cambridge

University and *The Economist*, people's faith in democracy is at an all-time low. Likewise, prior to Russia's launch of the war against Ukraine, the rise of political extremism in Hungary and Poland were symptoms of dissatisfaction with democracy. Democracy was dealt a further blow during the early days of the pandemic, with what was perceived by many as the relative success in dealing with that crisis by autocratic regimes such as that of Xi Jinping in China. Thanks to the speedy development of effective vaccines by companies in the West, often with help by leading universities, and their subsequent rapid rollout, coupled with the impacts on China's economy of Xi Jinping's lockdowns, much of this criticism has faded; but there was a time when the leading democracies such as the U.S., the UK, and the European Union, were seen as having handled the crisis particularly badly relative to China.

The fourth complex adaptive system in crisis is the global climate. Whilst any individual extreme weather or climate-related event is of course an isolated incident and one cannot conclude anything from that (climate is what you expect whereas weather is what you get), the increasing number and pattern of extreme weather events is building a statistical case which incontrovertibly is in support of the scientific argument that climate change is real, is not just random statistical seasonal variation, and has been caused by human economic activity since the beginning of the industrial revolution. By now, the science supporting man-made climate change driven by the release of greenhouse gases since the dawn of the industrial age is pretty solid.

Once again, looking at just one of these four systems in isolation and treating it as independent of the others won't work. Wholesale abandonment of the use of fossil fuels would cause economic devastation in much of the world, impacting in particular the poorest people, because the infrastructure to support renewable energy sources has not yet been built out sufficiently, as shown in the chart on the following page. Moreover, given China's role as the world's largest emitter of greenhouse gases, and showing absolutely no sign of doing anything to reduce its own emissions, all that the attempts by the U.S. and Europe to reduce their emissions will achieve is to impoverish their own people to China's relative benefit. All four of these complex adaptive systems need to be tackled together to find the best (in reality the least-bad) solution; a situation which would challenge even the best brains of scientists, philosophers, economists, and political thinkers.

Global primary energy consumption by source

Our World in Data

Primary energy is calculated based on the 'substitution method' which takes account of the inefficiencies in fossil fuel production by converting non-fossil energy into the energy inputs required if they had the same conversion losses as fossil fuels.

◻ Relative

160,000 TWh

140,000 TWh

120,000 TWh

100,000 TWh

80,000 TWh

60,000 TWh

40,000 TWh

20,000 TWh

0 TWh

1800   1850   1900   1950   2021

Other renewables
Modern biofuels
Solar
Wind
Hydropower
Nuclear
Natural gas

Oil

Coal

Traditional biomass

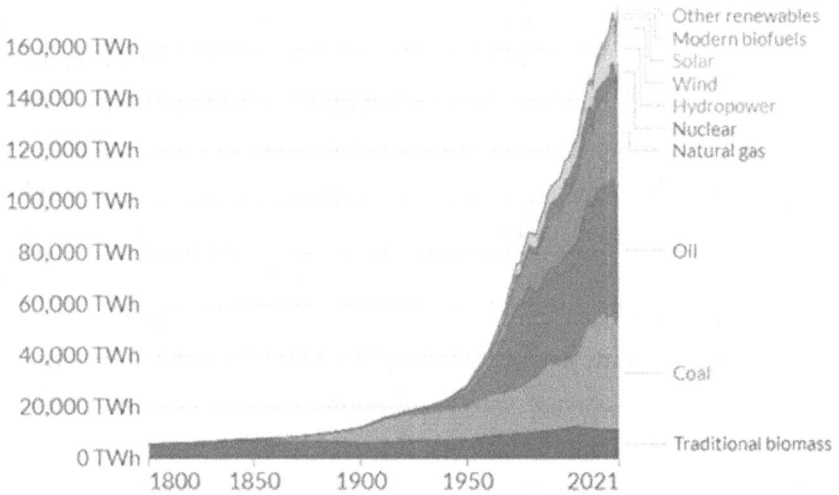

Source: Our World in Data based on Vaclav Smil (2017) and BP Statistical Review of World Energy
OurWorldInData.org/energy • CC BY

▶ 1800 ○━━━━━━━━━━━━━━━━━━━━━━━━━○ 2021

CHAPTER TWO:

IN DEFENSE OF DEMOCRACY

Our political leaders are required to make decisions which will impact our future within a framework of complex adaptive systems in which the future is fundamentally unknowable and in which actions may have outcomes which are completely unpredictable. In these circumstances, no matter how well-intentioned our leaders may be, ultimately, they are bound to fail. Whilst smart (or just lucky), politicians may have a run of decision making which turns out well; but eventually luck will run out for even the smartest politicians, and they will make decisions which, with the benefit of hindsight, will turn out to have been mistakes. Political power is very seductive, so whilst a politician's luck is rolling, they will continue to remain in power; but eventually their luck will run out, resulting in the observation of the British politician Enoch Powell that all political careers end in failure. Moreover, one of the tragedies of political leadership is that those individuals most desperate to achieve power are the ones least fit to exercise it. Perhaps leadership would be best thrust onto those who want it least, although the decisions made would be no better.

Knowing that all political leaders are destined ultimately to fail, it becomes of paramount importance to a country's citizens to have a means of pressing the reset button to allow policy actions to take a new direction. Often quite soon after we have voted, we may have cause for regret for voting the way we did and wish we had done otherwise. The beauty of democracy is that when the inevitable occurs, we have a peaceful means of removing the failed politicians from office. The ability to "throw the bums out" is cathartic and helps to expunge our guilt. Of course, when we vote in the next election, we know that we will simply be replacing one set of bums with another, who will go on to fail in their own way, and we will want to remove them, too, in due course; but this feature of democracy is a natural release-valve to peacefully reduce societal tensions. Of all the elements which are generally present in modern democracies: citizen involvement in decision making with some degree of equality between citizens who are granted a degree of liberty, a system of representation, majority rule, the rule of law, etc., ensuring a peaceful transition of power from one set of elected leaders to another is the single most important one.

In contrast, in an autocracy, the dictatorial leader will make mistakes just as in a democracy, but without a peaceful means of removing them they are likely to double-down on their mistakes, becoming ever more repressive and tyrannical. Countries ruled by an autocrat are therefore much more likely than democracies to be pushed to the extremes of revolution, civil war, and to wage war on their neighbors.

There are those who are seduced by the idea of a benign dictator; an altruistic individual whose self-abnegation will allow them to make wise decisions for the greater good, and whose decisions will benefit from their being made speedily, without the messy debate and procrastination to which democracies are prone. But these people delude themselves. The likelihood of decisions being made which, even in the most well-intentioned circumstances, subsequently turn out to have been suboptimal lead to no less an accumulation of errors, and a need for society to try a different route, but without a mechanism to effect it.

For this reason, I believe that it is right for the United States, as the leader of the free world, to encourage democracy to flourish everywhere, to increase the likelihood of peace for all. Moreover, I do not believe that democratic nations should treat non-democratic countries as peers at international organizations such as the United Nations and the G20. Toleration of autocracies and their treatment as equally valid political systems will, in my view, inevitably and ultimately lead to war.

Numerous global studies of the health of democratic politics show increasing dissatisfaction among citizens of developed countries over the last twenty years, and democracy has come under severe pressure in countries such as the United Kingdom and the United States. However, for all its messiness, its indecisiveness, its weak compromises and inefficiencies, and its tendency to throw up as leaders people who can think on their feet and produce witty answers presented slickly in a few snappy soundbites rather than people of deep intellect, nevertheless, democracy remains, as Winston Churchill famously described: *"the worst form of Government except for all those other forms that have been tried from time to time."* Those of us lucky enough to live in democratic countries should appreciate the fact and should do everything in our power to protect and nurture democracy; everything from the simple act of voting in every election in which we are eligible to resisting at all costs undemocratic practices such as gerrymandering (a process common in the U.S. in which politicians select their voters rather than the other way around), illegitimately denying the right to vote, and denying rights to free speech and independent news media.

Recognizing that democracy is the least-bad form of organizing a political framework, what should the world's leading democracies do? Over recent years, we have experienced deep undermining of democracy in many countries, including the United States and the United Kingdom – two countries at the very heart of liberal democracy. The United States is fortunate in having a set of Founding Fathers who were very wise when structuring their new country in the late eighteenth century, and in giving it robust political institutions, including, most importantly, a constitution. The Fathers knew that it would be impossible to set in stone a collection of rules which could remain immutable forever, yet still govern the country wisely. Although they couldn't couch it in terms of adaptivity as we now can, they nevertheless knew that the country they were creating would change over time in ways they could not foresee, so they had the wisdom to put in place a written constitution, but to make it possible to amend it as needed as society adapted, but only with some difficulty and a high bar to make changes.

In contrast, the United Kingdom does not have a written constitution, but instead the government operates according to a set of well-established precedents and protocols, which has been described as the "good chaps" theory of government. This has served Britain well for hundreds of years as senior parliamentarians and ministers, Members of Parliament and the Whitehall Civil Service, and, most importantly, the Prime Minister, have, for the most part, been "good chaps." But when the country has the misfortune to elect as its leaders the run of incompetents, cads, and bounders that it has seen in recent years, the foundations of Britain's democracy have been duly shaken to the core, and the lack of a written constitution has been laid bare by threats such as that to prorogue Parliament.

Loss of faith in democracy in recent years has been caused by many factors, but the principal reason is the stalling of income growth for the middle classes and the feeling that too much of the growing economic pie is being captured by a small, elite, protected class of citizens rather than being shared more equitably among all the people in a country. Causes of this feeling include globalization, which has seen many workers in democratic countries lose their livelihoods and suffer a standard of living no better, and in many cases much worse, than did their parents, resulting from the offshoring and outsourcing of jobs to China and other countries with much lower labor costs. Whilst all consumers have benefitted from the lower cost of goods resulting from globalization, and the lifting out of poverty of the millions in the countries to which the jobs were outsourced, should not be ignored. Not enough was done to help the people thrown out of work in industrialized countries by globalization. Had our political and corporate leaders been wise, they would have ensured that those who were benefiting most from globalization made sufficient transfer payments (essentially through the taxation system) to those who were losing out; but inevitably their greed exceeded their wisdom. I am reminded of the dictum of the fifth century BCE Chinese philosopher Confucius:

The noble man does what is right; the lesser man does what is profitable.

What if we had the wisdom of Confucius?

Beyond globalization, wealth disparity increased particularly as a result of the Global Financial Crisis of 2007–2009 in which policymakers' actions were seen by the general public to have bailed-out Wall Street whilst Main Street took the hit. I shall discuss in some detail in a later chapter the errors in these actions, and suggest what would have been a much wiser course; but for now it is sufficient to say that the events of those years, and their aftermath, demonstrated that our leaders had feet of clay, and that the fruits of our economy were not being shared fairly, but were being grabbed by the elite class of politicians, bankers, and corporate leaders. Up until the Crisis, we were accepting of the idea that those who contribute most to the generation of wealth; the brilliant inventors and entrepreneurs who risked penury by maxing-out borrowing on their credit card in order to back their idea, for example, should become billionaires if their creations enjoyed great success. But what stuck in the craw was that very ordinary talent, which created little of great benefit to society, accumulated for itself a disproportionate share of society's wealth. Political action in response to the crisis demonstrated that democratic capitalism as practiced in the U.S. today resulted in the privatization of profits, but also the socialization of losses. That people like the overpaid bankers and others with privileged positions in society, who lorded it over us, should be protected by the actions of the political class and the central banks, was, above all, what has driven political polarization in the world's leading democracies, and has driven the loss of faith in both democracy and capitalism.

This is particularly unfortunate because liberal democracy and capitalism have been responsible for all the progress in improving peoples' standard of living, health and longevity. For most of the entire existence of humanity, life was a struggle amidst squalor and ill health to find enough food to survive; life was, in Hobbes' memorable phrase: *nasty, brutish and short*. And no matter how wealthy one was, nor one's position in society, there wasn't much difference in standard of living, health, nor longevity; by modern standards, life was tough for all. Demonstrably modern alternatives to capitalism which have been tried, such as socialism and communism, have failed dismally for reasons I explain in the next chapter. So, for the benefit of all humanity, it is imperative that democracy and capitalism be preserved. And as for the privileged, for their own sake, they should see that it is in their long-term interest to share the blessings of our economy more equally. Historically, the pendulum of wealth disparity has never swung unceasingly in one direction, and usually its reversal is driven by calamitous events such as war and revolution. It would be much wiser for the elite to preempt such an outcome.

But recognizing that our democracy is imperfect and that it would be wise to ameliorate demonstrably unfair outcomes in order to protect the core principle is insufficient. The mechanism I have described explains why autocracies are to be feared and every opportunity should be taken to neutralize them. To be clear, our disagreement is not with the people of China, Russia, Iran, nor North Korea, as examples. People are people the world over, all with the same hopes, fears, and dreams. Rather, our issue is with the autocratic leaders of these countries who oppress sizeable factions of their own people and command the heights of their economies to direct their fruits towards wholly nefarious ends, whether that be as kleptocrats, simply to keep themselves in power indefinitely, to subjugate their own people, or to wage war on their neighbors.

It is simply not good enough for the United States to turn its back on these issues and to turn inwards. I can understand the desire, especially of those who have lost loved ones in Iraq or Afghanistan, for example, to say that America has spilled too much of its sons' and daughters' blood, and that we have spent more than enough treasure, for apparently little gain and less thanks, in defending or trying to instill democracy in other lands. We may well have had our fill of the rest of the world, but we would be naïve to think that the autocrats and despots have had enough of us, and that if we leave them alone, they will leave us alone. As I shall explain in the following chapter, capitalism is the best form of economic organization because it has at its root the same underlying mechanism. Capitalism and liberal democracy go hand-in-hand. Although through mismanagement and misguided attempts to rectify what were perceived shortcomings, America has done much over the years to damage its economic potential, and yet it remains the world's strongest economy; and as long as America does not allow its democracy and its capitalist market economics to further deteriorate, it will remain the strongest economic and military power. There will therefore always be other countries whose leaders are jealous of America's power and wealth, and who will seek to undermine us.

I can also understand the frustration of those who see wealthy European countries such as Germany not pay their fair share towards NATO and for their own defense. Germany and several other European countries have long parasitized U.S. taxpayers. This is as a result of a perennial problem with moral hazard. Because Germany knows that it is in the U.S.'s interest to protect western Europe from Russian aggression in order to prevent Russia from ever becoming sufficiently powerful that it might one day threaten the U.S., Germany knows that when push comes to shove, the United States will always defend Europe. Having this insurance policy in its back pocket, Germany therefore feels able to depend on that U.S. protection, and doesn't bother to pay the fees to NATO which it is obliged to by treaty, nor does it adequately spend on its own defense. Although this situation has been ongoing for a very long time, President Trump was the first U.S. President to call-out the Germans and other European countries on this issue.

Far from accepting autocrats as perfectly acceptable leaders of countries with equally valid political systems, we should recognize the threats which these dictators present. As leader of the free world America should join with the globe's other liberal democracies: the European Union, Japan, South Korea, India, the United Kingdom, Canada, Australia, New Zealand, and the democratic countries of Latin America to seek to overthrow undemocratic regimes everywhere.

America's unsuccessful military forays, from as long ago as Korea and Vietnam, and more recently in Iraq and Afghanistan, have given the idea of regime-change a bad name. That these attempts to extend democracy failed is incontrovertible, but we should not let these failures blind us to the good intent behind them. Nor should we forget the tremendous successes of regime change led by America after the Second World War in Germany and Japan. Perhaps it is the case that the reason regime change in these cases was successful was because the effects of war had so destroyed the will of those peoples that the Germans and Japanese were grateful for war's end and saw the Americans as their liberators from their own despotic leaders. Perhaps the peoples' suffering at the hands of Saddam and of the Taliban in Iraq and Afghanistan was insufficient for them to see America as their liberator; but whilst George W. Bush's efforts were ultimately unsuccessful, we should recognize that his aims were noble.

This is not a call for America to wage war upon China, Russia, Iran, and North Korea. Like all reasonable people, I want peace; but in the words of the great fifth century Chinese military strategist Sun Tzu: *"If you want peace, prepare for war."* Even with its superior military might, America is not strong enough to take on these powers simultaneously.

Instead, America should play a long game, leveraging its soft power to the full in attempting to convert the young people of these countries to a belief in liberal democracy and capitalism as delivering a superior standard of living for all citizens. Given time, it may be hoped that the populations of these countries, with help from the liberal democracies, may be able to overturn their current regimes by themselves.

To aid in this struggle, the liberal democracies should seek to withdraw from economic entanglement with the autocracies. Clearly this is easier said than done and may take many years, but the liberal democracies should set a course with this aim. David Ricardo in the early nineteenth century explained in his theory of comparative advantage why free trade confers great benefits upon those participating in it. In principle, based purely upon an economic argument, free trade, including the autocracies as well as the liberal democracies, would lead to enhanced economic well-being; but this is a case where the imperative of advancing the cause of liberal democracy itself trumps the economic benefits of free trade. Consequently, the liberal democracies should remove all trade barriers between themselves, thereby helping them all to strengthen their economies, but deliberately exclude all the autocracies from membership of the free-trade club. To the greatest extent possible, they should seek to substitute the imported energy, commodities, and goods they currently import from the autocracies with similar material from within their own club. We may expect that the club of autocracies will seek to do the same for themselves, to strengthen their own economies; but since the aggregate economic output of the autocracies is already smaller than that of the democracies, and the generally capitalist economies of the latter produce superior economic growth than do those of the autocracies, over time this bifurcation of the world into two blocs will lead to increasing dispersion in economic well-being between the two. Weaker countries which at the outset chose to join the club of autocracies are likely to gradually peel off and seek to join the club of democracies due to the superior economic performance of the latter. Provided that they accept the requirement to adopt full democratic principles and adhere to the same, they should be allowed to join. At the same time, the club of democracies should continually police its own members to make sure that there is no backsliding in their adherence to democratic practices.

Over time, this will see a continual strengthening of the club of democracies and a relative weakening of the autocracies until a point may be reached at which the remaining autocratic governments are overthrown by their own people, or the overwhelming relative military strength of the club of democracies allows them to force regime change upon the remaining recalcitrant and impose democratic constitutions upon them. Although I see this as the best strategy to achieve long term peace, I am not so naïve as to think that it is without risks. Clearly as the autocrats' power weakens over time, those amongst them who are nuclear-armed may see the use of their weapons as a best, last-gasp strategy for survival, and that the course I am proposing will accelerate this threat. But the threat of their use of these weapons is ever with us, and the democracies cannot allow themselves to be blackmailed in this way; to do so would only prolong the continued threat which the autocrats pose. Likewise, the democracies will always be vulnerable to the threat of terrorism, either from disaffected members of their own communities or from external groups within the autocracies, such as Al Qaeda did in the early 2000s. Again, threats of this kind are always with us and nothing the democracies can do will alleviate these risks. We have already tried extending the hand of friendship to the likes of China and to Russia, but we can see today that these attempts simply have not worked. The idea that all political regimes are equally valid and why can't we all just get along together, holding hands around the campfire and singing "Kumbaya", is hopelessly naïve.

When Richard Nixon and Henry Kissinger extended the hand of friendship to China in 1972, doubtless it was primarily because they sought to establish China as an ally of the U.S. during the Cold War against the Soviet Union. The thought that this might ultimately lead to the opening up of China to take its place in the world's club of democracies was only of secondary importance. Over time, there was a hope that China would liberalize. China was admitted into the World Trade Organization and given a seat at the security council of the United Nations. Senior leaders and businesspeople actively encouraged trade between the West and China, which, given China's much lower labor costs, helped in reducing inflation during the period known as the Great Moderation, albeit at the cost of gutting much of the U.S.'s and Europe's manufacturing industries. At the time when these outreaches were made, it was reasonable to hope that China was on a path to democracy, and had China proceeded down that path, then the pain borne by those who lost their jobs due to globalization might have been worth it in terms of a more peaceful geopolitical environment. But with the accession of the current leader Xi Jinping, it is now clear that these hopes have been dashed. Whilst Mr. Xi understandably wants to increase China's economic might and speaks of China's "peaceful rise" through his actions, he has made clear that he is bent on far more than that. Xi has abandoned the cautious words of Deng Xiaoping (adopted in turn from Sun Tzu): *"Hide your strength, bide your time."* We would be naïve not to recognize that Mr. Xi seeks to avenge China's "century of humiliation": the subjugation of the Qing dynasty by the European powers, especially the British and the Japanese, between 1839 and 1949. Whilst we may regret the actions of European and Japanese imperialists in times past, we should nevertheless seek to block any attempt by China to seek vengeance.

Likewise, after the fall of the Soviet Union and the leadership of Mikhail Gorbachev, it was reasonable to hope that Russia and its former satellites might tread the path of democracy. Even in the early years of the current Russian leader Vladimir Putin, it was possible to believe that Russia too would establish a liberal democracy. But sadly, it was not to be. Like Xi Jinping, Putin too regrets the humiliation of the Soviet Union, which he regards as the greatest geopolitical disaster of the twentieth century. Russia has a long history of invasion via the North European plain, most recently by Napoleon in 1812 and by Hitler in 1941; but this does not excuse Putin's desire to recreate the strategic depth which the leadership in Moscow during the days of the Soviet Union enjoyed by subjugating a chain of satellite vassal states down its western flank. Like Xi, Putin should at all costs be resisted by the West.

At the time of this writing, there are those who see Putin's failing war against Ukraine and suggest that he be given an "off-ramp"; a means of negotiating a peace treaty which will cease the fighting and allow Putin's forces to withdraw from Ukraine (at least from the territory taken by Russia since the war began in February 2022, if not also the Crimea and southeastern Ukraine territory taken in the invasion beginning in 2014), thereby allowing Putin to save face. This is a deeply mistaken strategy, for Putin would use such an accord as a time to regroup and rebuild the strength of his armed forces in order to mount more assaults later. Moreover, Xi Jinping, the Iranian ayatollahs, and Kim Jong Un, are also watching events. Xi is convinced that the American setbacks in Iraq and Afghanistan, and the increasing political polarization and wealth disparity in the U.S. are symptomatic of the country's terminal decline. He has made it clear that he is girding for war and will attempt to take Taiwan by force within the next few years. American acceptance of territorial gains made by Russia in Ukraine would be taken as further signs of American weakness and would accelerate Xi's plans. As well as simply being the right and moral thing to do, it is in America's best interest to see Putin be utterly humiliated in Ukraine and that Russia is not only forced to give up its territorial gains since 2022, but is also forced to relinquish Crimea and territory taken in the southeast.

On a per-capita basis as well as in absolute terms, Russia is virtually a third-world country. Despite its huge landmass, much of which is inaccessible and unproductive, Russia's population is rapidly aging and declining, suffering from alcoholism and poor health. Corruption is endemic, leading to poor productivity and weak economic growth. Were it not for its nuclear arsenal, the West could safely ignore Russia and see Vladimir Putin as little more than Xi Jinping's lapdog. However, Putin sees himself as a modern-day Peter the Great with territorial and military ambitions to match. Beyond increasing Moscow's strategic depth by putting more distance between Moscow and the NATO front line, Ukraine is not important to Putin in and of itself. It is merely the most convenient playing field on which Putin may exercise his ambitions. Putin cares nothing for either the Russian or the Ukrainian people; they are merely the price he is willing to pay for his ambitions.

Although much wealthier and more powerful than Russia, China too with its huge, although now also declining, population, is, on a per capita basis, a third world country. Thanks to the one child policy and the resulting sex imbalance, given parents' preference for sons and selective abortion, China is now also aging rapidly. It has been widely commented that China will grow old before it grows rich, and for all the commentary that, on current trends, China's GDP will at some point outstrip that of the U.S., it remains to be seen if this will in fact be the case. Xi Jinping certainly sees it as his destiny to avenge the Chinese for the century of humiliation and is building his military capabilities on land and in the South China sea with a view to taking Taiwan – long regarded by China as part of its sovereign territory. Xi has announced it as his plan to ready his military capabilities to be ready to mount an attack on Taiwan within the next five years, doubtless aware that China's economic strength is likely to peak within this timescale due to its falling population, so he needs to move ahead rapidly to maximize the opportunity this may present to him.

Xi Jinping and Vladimir Putin have declared their aim to seek a multi-polar world, replacing the World Order set in place by the U.S. after the Second World War, and wrestling power from a United States they see as being in decline. Were all the poles in a multi-polar world held by liberal democracies then such a situation might be acceptable – it would probably not be so different from the world order in place since the fall of the Soviet Union – but that is not what is on offer. The multi-polar world Xi seeks would see China impose one party rule of the Chinese Communist Party over the globe. China uses its newfound friendship with Russia to disguise its real aim, which is global CCP domination, by pretending that the multipolar world it seeks would indeed have multiple poles, including Russia and the U.S. In this goal, Xi sees Putin merely as what Vladimir Lenin referred to as a "useful idiot", complicit in his aims and a useful cover for some of his activities, but with absolutely no power and of no real consequence in Xi's grand scheme.

Without the strength to reliably defeat the combined military power of China and Russia, the United States must, together with the major liberal democracies, bide its time and play the long game, as I have described, leveraging their superior economic model to outgrow the autocracies, in the same way that Ronald Reagan's Star Wars strategy was largely responsible for bringing about the collapse of the Soviet Union. To understand this we must now turn our attention away from geopolitics and towards economics.

CHAPTER THREE:

IN DEFENSE OF CAPITALISM

That the success of democracy as a political model should be rooted in the idea of the inevitable failure of political leadership may sound paradoxical, but I believe it is in fact a quite widespread phenomenon, and the same mechanism which results in capitalism being the most successful economic system.

The phenomenal growth of businesses and the financial success of business founders such as the Tech industry entrepreneurs which we read about every day gives us the false impression that starting and growing a business is easy, but the financial media have an inherent bias towards writing about successful businesses. They will also write about spectacular business failures too, of course, but that is usually only after a business has first experienced great success and then has failed subsequently. The news media like nothing better than to gloat about the Icarus-like fall of a once-lauded business leader, but if instead you happen to be the unfortunate founder of a business which never got off the ground – which is the situation for the vast majority of would-be entrepreneurs who attempt to start a business – it's unlikely you would ever be invited to give the Harvard Commencement Address. So, whilst evidence of business success is all around us, the reality is that business is hard, and the overwhelming majority of business ventures fail within their first few years.

The beauty of capitalism is that it is a sifting mechanism which quickly kills off unsuccessful businesses without destroying too much capital, allowing sufficient capital to be preserved to be invested in the next generation of businesses, some of which will turn out to be successful and then propagate into the future. Eventually, these successful businesses too will succumb to competition and disruption from new entrants, whereby Schumpeterian creative destruction, which is the essence of a healthy capitalist economy, causes these too to fall by the wayside, in turn to be replaced by the still more-successful new businesses of the future.

In contrast, in a centrally planned, socialist, economy, those controlling the levers of economic power assume that their superior intellect and business acumen will allow them to pick winners, and this, coupled with the lowest cost borrowing power of the state, will ensure success. But committees of the-great-and-the-good are no better at backing winning ideas than is the typical entrepreneur, and the benefits of lowest cost financing and being led by the cream of the class of civil servants are not sufficient to overcome the weaknesses of the socialist model, not least because the latter are more interested in protecting their privileged employment than they are in serving the needs of customers. When state-run businesses fail, having the full weight of the state behind them, they destroy so much capital that there is insufficient left to invest in new ventures.

Historically, government industrial policy – the idea that government should back certain favored industries and "nudge" the economy in certain favored directions – has a dismal track record of failure. One might have hoped that by now governments would have learned their lesson; yet despite Albert Einstein's view, that the definition of insanity is to keep repeating the same action in expectation of a different result, governments around the world continue to implement industrial policies which go on to fall well short of their aims.

Capitalist economies so clearly out-performed centrally planned economies in the period after the Second World War that many countries which had flirted with socialism and had nationalized much of business, such as the United Kingdom, subsequently abandoned this model. Margaret Thatcher's championing of privatization of the formerly state-owned businesses in the UK in the 1980s unleashed the dynamism of a capitalist economy and became a role model for many other countries.

Unfortunately, socialism is rearing its head once more as a result of increasing wealth and income inequality. As Winston Churchill said: "*The inherent vice of capitalism is the unequal sharing of blessings. The inherent virtue of socialism is the equal sharing of miseries.*" I agree that increasing wealth disparity is a problem which society does need to deal with, because otherwise there is a risk that increasing social tensions cause the baby of capitalism to be thrown out with the bathwater of inequality, but industrial policies and more government intervention in the economy are not the answer.

Like the relative success of democracy as a political system, that the success of capitalism as an economic system should also be rooted ultimately in the failure of underlying processes may be thought paradoxical, but the fact that the two share this common trait is not coincidence; in fact, liberal democracy and capitalism go hand in hand. Unfortunately, the word "liberal" in the United States today has come to mean "socialist", but in its original usage, in the sense of the classical liberals of Victorian Britain, as espoused by political leaders of the time such as William Gladstone, it conveyed an essentially capitalist, libertarian political and economic outlook: being today what we would term socially liberal but fiscally conservative. Since that time however, the United States, Britain and much of the western world has strayed far from this path, especially since the growth of the welfare state resulting from actions taken in response to the Great Depression by

President Franklin Roosevelt and President Lyndon Johnson's Great Society reforms, and other, more recent, economic and financial crises, but the path of liberal democracy is one to which the United States and indeed all countries should seek to return. Not least this is because the mechanism underlying the success of democracy and capitalism is truly fundamental and extends even to the development of life on earth itself.

To see why this is the case consider Charles Darwin's theory of evolution. Darwin's idea of "the survival of the fittest" is often misinterpreted to mean the survival of the strongest, but in using the word "fittest" Darwin meant those organisms most-fitted or best-adapted for the environment in which they found themselves. Although the mechanism wasn't understood at the time, we now know that evolution occurs because as the DNA within cells is replicated before they multiply, allowing the organism of which the cells form a part to grow, the replication is frequently imperfect and subject to random mutations. Most of those random errors lead to features which, when expressed within the organism, are deleterious, and, since they give the organism no benefits, they are not passed onto future generations. However, sometimes those mutations lead to characteristics which result in the organism being better adapted to its surroundings, and in this case, since the organism now has an advantage over competitors without those characteristics, these are passed onto future generations.

Were an organism perfectly matched to its environment, and the environment immutable, then any changes in its genetic makeup resulting from random mutations in DNA replication would only ever be damaging. But in a situation where the environment changes periodically, perfect replication of DNA from one generation of cells to the next would result in the organism being locked into a genetic makeup which, over time, would be increasingly unsuited to its environment, and as a result it would most likely die. Even though the majority of random mutations in DNA replication will likely be damaging, it is precisely those mutations which confer some advantage in allowing the organism to be better suited to its new environment as that environment changes, which allow the organism to evolve and continue to prosper. The evolutionary winnowing process which allows those organisms with the genetic makeup best adapted to their environment to propagate forward to the next generation, whilst the less-well adapted are out-competed and fall by the wayside, is exactly analogous to the winnowing process by which capitalism provides the best economic framework and democracy the best political framework.

That the success of such apparently disparate systems as democracy, capitalism, and life on earth itself should all fundamentally be rooted in the concept of failure in the underlying process is profound; but this underlying symmetry is ultimately the reason why democracy, for all its frustrations, is the best form of political organization for a people, and why capitalism, for all its imperfections, is the best economic model.

Note that my argument does not claim that democratic government is always perfect, or even good, just as capitalism, too, has failings. *"Out of the crooked timber of humanity no straight thing was ever wrought"* is an idea first espoused by Immanuel Kant in his book *Idea for a General History with a Cosmopolitan Purpose*, published in 1784. Indeed, no human may claim to be perfect; we all have strengths and weaknesses, as do the constructs which humans develop, such as political and economic frameworks. But whilst democracy and capitalism are both imperfect, in their respective fields they are both infinitely better than anything else. It was this that led Winston Churchill to say: *"Democracy is the worst possible form of government, apart from all the other forms which have been tried from time to time".*

The evolutionary mechanism, too, has its flaws. Most anatomists would argue that if they were starting from scratch, they could design a human knee joint which would be simpler and less vulnerable to injury than the one which evolution has bequeathed to us. Likewise, until after the Second World War, the condition of the overwhelming majority of humanity during the entire existence of Homo *sapiens* on our planet, even those living in the richest countries, was one of hunger and deprivation.

Only with the scientific advances of genetics pioneers such as those by plant breeder Norman Borlaug, who developed strains of wheat and other grains to increase crop yields by orders of magnitude, did global hunger subside. It is now widely recognized that the global obesity epidemic which much of the rich world is suffering from is caused by humans' genetic makeup which is programmed to store energy in the body in the form of fat during times of plentiful food in anticipation of leaner times ahead since that was humanity's condition for most of our existence. Now that we live in a world of plenty, that genetic makeup which was designed to ensure survival in times of famine has turned from an asset into a liability. Eventually, our genetic makeup will adapt to the changes in our circumstances, so long as plentiful food sources remain available, but that could take a while.

That the environment in which life flourishes should be one in which adaptations of all living organisms occur, in conjunction with an environment which itself changes in unpredictable ways, is of philosophical interest. One can imagine constructing the possible arrangements in a simple 2 X 2 matrix. On one axis of the matrix, we have the environment: either it is immutable or else it changes. On the other axis we have all of life: either it is capable of mutating and adapting or it is not. The two off-diagonal elements: living organisms which cannot adapt in an environment which changes, or alternatively living organisms which do mutate over time, living in an environment which is immutable; are unviable. In either of these cases, life cannot survive. The only states of the world which are viable are the diagonal matrix elements. The one viable state: living organisms which are immutable and are perfectly matched to an environment which is also immutable, is stable and sustainable indefinitely, although one wonders how such a situation could ever arise. The probability that such a finely tuned universe would ever be created is vanishingly small and would surely require one to invoke the hand of God. The fact that the world we live in corresponds to the other diagonal element of the matrix: the one in which the environment changes in unpredictable ways, but in which living organisms mutate and can therefore adapt to the changing environment, is surely reassuring. This is the world in which we find ourselves precisely because it's the only world in which life could possibly exist; a manifestation of the anthropic principle, first proposed by Robert Dicke in 1957.

The relative success of democracy, capitalism and evolution in relation to their respective alternatives may be likened to an attempt to move from one end to the other of a huge windowless warehouse with no lighting, stacked with large randomly placed boxes which can move around autonomously. We enter through the door at one end of the warehouse, which closes behind us, leaving us completely in the dark. We are told that there is a door at the other end through which we can exit, and our task is to traverse from the door through which we enter at one end to the door at the other end, and to arrive safely, in one piece. Autocracy and central planning are akin to the leader deciding upon which course we should follow and in the entire party charging full-tilt in the chosen direction, with disastrous results as we collide with one or more of the boxes.

The way of democracy, capitalism and evolution, in contrast, is to gingerly feel our way forwards, trying this way and that, with lots of false-starts and our finding ourselves in many a blind alley, causing us to retrace our steps. As frustrating as this process is, however, it will ultimately allow us to cross safely to the other side, uninjured save for a few bruises and the odd stubbed toe.

We must condition ourselves and recognize that any attempt to improve upon the outcomes of democracy, capitalism or evolution by tinkering with their inner workings will only make things worse; such attempts are doomed to fail. Instead of trying to improve on any of them it is much more effective simply to leave them alone but to address the negative outcomes which each of them produces.

The desire to interfere with the pure approach to capitalism is particularly attractive to politicians, who believe that they can steal from one area of the economy and distribute the proceeds to another in an attempt to buy votes. But attempts to add bells and whistles to capitalism in order to mitigate perceived shortcomings act like barnacles on the bottom of the boat, increasing drag and preventing its smooth passage through the water. Eventually, the accumulation becomes so great that the boat is in danger of capsizing and sinking, with us in it. Our approach to capitalism in the United States is approaching this dangerous condition. The best move at this point would be to scrape-off all the barnacles and begin our journey anew; refreshed and reinvigorated.

CHAPTER FOUR:

IN PRAISE OF DIVERSITY

The complex adaptive nature of society which underpins democracy and capitalism also drives the need for diversity in successful enterprises. Diversity has come to the fore in recent years as a key issue upon which corporate boards and executive management should focus, owing to the fact that women and people of color, in particular, have been severely under-represented at senior levels for a very long time. Of course, women and people of color are every bit as capable of performing in the C-suite and boardroom as are white men, but historically they have been under-represented purely as a result of sexism and racism; and by the fact that by excluding more than half the population from consideration, a white man more-than doubles his chance of landing that promotion or board seat.

Belatedly, companies are beginning to address the issues which have led women and people of color to be unfairly discriminated against, but the so-called Diversity programs adopted by so many corporations would more correctly be given the fuller title of Diversity, Equity and Inclusion (DEI) because in fact their programs typically address only two factors – sex and skin-color – not true diversity in all its richness. These two factors are among the suite of characteristics protected under U.S. employment law, alongside national origin, religion, pregnancy, disability, age and citizenship status, and certainly need to be addressed given historic under-representation, but focusing on just these two addresses issues mainly of equity and inclusion. True diversity has many more facets than just these two, and forward-thinking organizations need to embrace real diversity as a factor driving business success, not just as a matter of equity and inclusion, important though they are.

If the operating environments of governments, businesses and other organizations were immutable then diversity would not be important as a success-driver (although it would still be important from the perspectives of fairness and inclusion). For example, in an immutable environment a company whose board and senior executives were optimally selected to perform best in that environment – essentially cultural clones – would continue to be the optimal set indefinitely, and any changes to the optimal set would, by definition, worsen performance. But, of course, the business environment is not immutable; it is constantly evolving, and changing in ways that are fundamentally impossible to predict. In such an environment the groupthink of a monocultural leadership team is likely to result in its being blindsided. It is for this reason that a wise company insists upon great diversity amongst its board and senior executive ranks; so as to be more agile and more capable of adapting quickly to meet the demands of the rapidly changing environment in which it operates.

To be sure, even a thoroughly diverse senior team may fail to adapt sufficiently or fast enough – in business there are no guarantees of success – but having a senior team which consists of a monoculture is surely setting-up a company to fail. In contrast, having a cohesive and well-functioning but truly diverse leadership team will give a company its best chance of long-term success. That so many organizations claim to have diversity programs and hire Chief Diversity Officers, but in fact to focus only on the two protected characteristics of sex and skin color tells us that they neither understand the real value of diversity nor particularly like it. These organizations have jumped on the diversity bandwagon but are just going through the motions; wanting to be seen to be in compliance with societal norms by being able to check the diversity box; but their diversity agenda in reality is just tokenism.

It doesn't even help the people they purport to. Over-promoting someone into a role for which they are unsuited just because they meet diversity criteria is setting up that individual to fail, setting-back the cause of true diversity. You may be sure that plenty of people in the anti-woke lobby made hay of the fact that the board of Silicon Valley Bank had a full complement of diverse individuals, and that the San Francisco Federal Reserve supervisory oversight team had held so many meetings with the board and senior executive team about climate change (Environmental, Social and Governance, or ESG, being yet another three-letter acronym bandwagon alongside the DEI bandwagon so beloved of woke management consultants and other executive-guru busybodies), but apparently no one had the wit to focus on basic banking hygiene such as asset-liability management and interest rate risk management.

President Joe Biden also made a rookie mistake when appointing a new Justice to the bench of the U.S. Supreme Court by announcing first and foremost that he was going to appoint a woman of color, and then subsequently nominated Ketanji Brown Jackson for the role. Ms. Brown Jackson is eminently qualified to serve, and I am sure she will go on to have a distinguished career on the bench, but because of the way in which the announcement was made, at the back of her mind there must always be a nagging doubt: *I don't really deserve to be here on merit; the only reason that I am here is that I am a black woman.* To undermine Ms. Brown Jackson in this way was extremely foolish. A more enlightened path for President Biden to have followed would have been for him to announce instead that he was going to nominate the very best candidate for the role that he could possibly find. He should then have performed an exhaustive search, at the end of which he should have nominated Ketanji Brown Jackson. The end result would have been the same, but how much more empowering would it have been for Ms. Brown Jackson, knowing that the reason she was nominated was because she was simply the best?

CHAPTER FIVE:

GOVERNMENT – A HOPELESS TASK

Recognizing that political leaders are doomed to make mistakes, and that central planning is doomed to fail, our natural instincts should be to have government do as little as possible, devolving decision-making authority to the lowest possible levels of the political hierarchy, and with as much as possible being left to families and individuals to decide for themselves. Indeed, such was the philosophy of the founding fathers of the United States who were fearful of an over-mighty central government, and who believed that power be conferred upon government by the people. The fathers believed that the powers so conferred should be enumerated (i.e., limited in number), and that the government should be able to exercise only those powers prescribed within the limits. Powers not so conferred should reside still with the states and with the people.

Whilst there may be some people who believe that they are so incompetent that they would rather delegate the running of their lives to someone else, the overwhelming majority of us would rather be masters of our own fate and believe that we know better than anyone else how to spend our own money and time. Whilst it is reasonable to accept that people need a degree of maturity and experience before they can be expected to make sensible decisions, so that babies and young children may be reliant upon their families for an extended period, I suspect most of us instinctively feel that the mature individual and the family unit are the most appropriate levels at which most decisions should be made.

Yet there are some types of decisions which need to be made collectively at higher levels in the hierarchy within a polity: defense of the nation; enforcement of the rule of law governing the relations between society's members; important infrastructure developed for the benefit of the common good, such as transport networks; the standardization of weights and measures discussed earlier, and so on, are examples which come to mind; but such cases should be limited to those which clearly impact large swathes of society and for which it would be deeply inefficient and risk conflicting and contradictory results to atomize the decision making process to too great an extent. The key is to identify the nature of the problem and the system in which it operates in order to determine whether a centralized or wisdom-of-crowds approach to decision making is better.

Without the language of complex adaptive systems and an intellectual understanding of these factors, it may be thought remarkable that humanity has stumbled, apparently by accident, upon these techniques. After all, democracy is thought to have been first developed in ancient Athens around the fifth century BCE, and capitalism emerged naturally out of the industrial revolution of the late eighteenth century. But when you consider the common underlying element; that of the success of the overarching framework being rooted in the failure of the underlying process, and that democracy and capitalism share this common trait with Darwinian evolution, its natural development does not seem so strange. It is rather the attempts to correct the processes of democracy and capitalism in order to produce what are perceived as fairer outcomes that has led to the utter failures observed in alternative approaches, such as autocracy, oligarchy, fascism, socialism, and communism.

The United States has moved a long way from the philosophy extant at its founding, which was much more closely aligned with capitalism and representative liberal democracy than it is today (albeit that the franchise was much more restricted then). Inevitably, there are episodic periods of crisis in any country's life which the government of the day uses as an excuse to arrogate ever more power unto itself: "Never let a crisis go to waste," as Winston Churchill put it. With the citizenry panicked by whatever has caused the crisis, it's not surprising that instinctively we look to how we may prevent it from happening again, and government, offering the balm of some emollient policy, takes advantage of the opportunity to extend its reach, reducing our freedoms in the process. Invariably, politicians call for increased regulation against the factors identified as the proximate causes of the crisis. But in practice, regulation is rarely the best answer to any of these situations and for all the well-intentioned actions of policymakers in attempting to address the causes of the last crisis, invariably the actions have the perverse effect of making the next crisis much worse. There are several factors at play which cause this.

For one thing, policymakers and regulators are perennially the generals who fought the last war, noisily slamming shut stable doors long after the horses had already bolted. Given the adaptive nature of markets, by the time regulators have gotten around to penning new rules to address perceived market failings, market participants have already licked their wounds and moved on. You may be sure those who were losing money would change their behavior and make sure they don't lose again. Of course, after a prolonged period of rule-writing, industry consultation and implementation, once the new rules have been adopted, market participants will adapt to them, too.

Dealing with the problem of adaptation would require eternal vigilance on the part of regulators and market supervisors, amending rules as emerging risks and practices evolved; but the most sharp-witted in society rarely take jobs as regulators; the compensation offered for such roles rarely reaches a level designed to attract the brightest and best. (To be clear, there are sharp-witted fellows amongst policymakers, but that is usually because they believe that they may benefit from their privileged position to grab more of the economic pie for themselves, at less risk, and by expending less effort than they would do from honest labor in the private sector.)

The schematic chart illustrated below shows the relative level of compensation paid for public sector and private sector jobs as a function of an individual's ability. Most of the talented people in our society crave recognition of their abilities, whether these be artistic, creative, entrepreneurial, intellectual, managerial, sporting, or whatever. They want to operate at the forefront of their field, not play second fiddle by reviewing and controlling the output of others. And society recognizes these factors, as the chart shows. There is very little discrimination in the level of compensation offered to employees in public sector jobs, regardless of how much or how little talent the employee has, with most promotions being driven instead by factors such as age and time served, which correlate very poorly with ability. In contrast, in the private sector, pay at the lowest end of the talent scale is very poor, whilst at the upper end, the sky's the limit. As a result, the most talented people go to work in the private sector where their abilities will be appropriately rewarded, whereas all of the least-talented people try to get government jobs where they will be paid more than the market-rate for their talent suggests they are worth, and from which it will be very hard to displace them, no matter how poor their productivity. This explains your typical experience at the DMV.

With these factors at play, it is naïve to suppose that regulators and supervisors, however diligent they may be, can police the actions of bankers, hedge fund managers, private equity players, and so on, whose compensation sits at a level which attracts some of the most talented people in the world. Not every individual is attracted by money, of course, but few people of real talent are so altruistic that they would spurn the riches on an offer in the private sector. Even those people who rise to the upper echelons of the civil service, after a lifetime spent in the public sector, seek to monetize their network and connections by taking private sector jobs after their retirement. It is often argued that some movement of people between the private and public sectors is a good thing as private sector experience will help to cross-fertilize ideas to the public sector; but a close inspection of those who claim private sector experience at some point in their career, for example, members of the Board of Governors of the Federal Reserve, reveal that most of their career service was spent in other public sector roles or in academia. Their very short stint in the private sector was when they leveraged their network of contacts by joining a private equity company, bank, or hedge fund as a senior advisor. You may be sure their time in the private sector was not spent on a trading desk nor in the nitty-gritty details of yield curve construction using B-spline functions.

Compensation as a Function of Skill Level

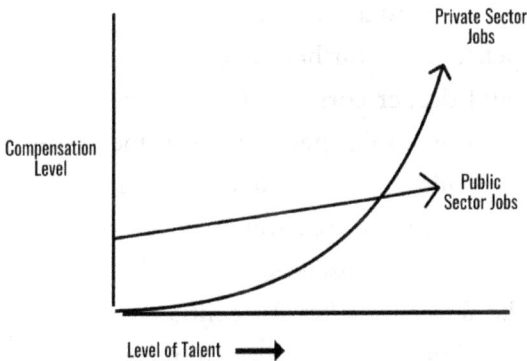

Private Sector Jobs

Compensation Level

Public Sector Jobs

Level of Talent ➡

With market participants and adaptive markets always one-step (or more) ahead of regulators, the question arises of what is their purpose, and are the consumers and taxpayers well-served by the huge expense of regulation, the costs of which are invariably passed through to consumers (and, in the case of catastrophic regulatory failure resulting in bank-bailouts, directly to taxpayers), as well as the costs of regulatory drag on innovation and productivity highlighted earlier?

But there is a philosophical question at the heart of regulation, too: to what extent should society protect its members, including even from their own stupidity? Certainly, we may regard it as the role of government to maintain a military force in order to protect citizens from attack by external threats, and emergency services such as the police to protect us from internal threats and to help uphold the rule of law, and a fire brigade and emergency health services to help citizens in their times of greatest distress when life may be threatened. But beyond provision of these basic services from which all members of society may benefit, libertarians would surely argue that each should be allowed to go to hell in their own handbasket; that to expect society collectively (in other words: taxpayers) to foot the bill for someone's naïve actions risks encouraging moral hazard; the idea that when someone is protected from the consequences of their actions by some form of insurance, they have no incentive to guard against risk. It is the clamor for protection at the public expense which further drives the extension of government into ever more and deeper corners of our lives, and which drives the proportion of national output spent on government ever higher, leaving taxpayers with less and less of their own money to spend or invest as they see fit. If instead people were allowed to suffer the negative consequences of their own mistakes, they would perhaps learn valuable lessons and make fewer mistakes. In contrast, society's toleration and bailing-out of stupid behavior only leads to more of it.

In the United States, historically we took the view that allowing people to take their own risks, including the risk of complete failure, was essential to a healthy, vibrant economy. Socialist-leaning nanny-states, in which people have much less freedom to take risks, in contrast, are usually far less efficient and productive, leaving everyone in society poorer. Over time, attempts to address the perceived failings of capitalist economies have inadvertently led to the destruction of everything upon which a successful economy depends, including the risk of failure and Schumpeterian creative destruction, resulting in increasing numbers of protected, zombie enterprises, declining productivity (and correspondingly, declining income growth), and ballooning fiscal deficits. Without the economic growth fostered by a truly capitalist economy, the United States and other liberal democracies will not be able to outgrow the authoritarian economies at a sufficiently rapid rate, stretching-out the time for which they will be vulnerable to attack by the authoritarians. As a matter of urgency, we should look to reinvigorate our capitalist economy by scraping from our (metaphorical) boat the socialist barnacles which have been allowed to proliferate in recent years, thereby dragging down our growth rate and holding us back from achieving our full potential.

The famed investors Warren Buffett and his Berkshire Hathaway partner Charlie Munger speak often about their interest in finding companies to invest in which have an "economic moat" which protects their earning power from competition. The moat may take the form of regulation, in highly regulated industries, such as banking, which, as explained by Berkshire Hathaway, has been a big investor in banks. Compliance with regulation is costly, which acts to prevent smaller banks competing with their larger brethren who can spread the costs of compliance over a much larger client base. The lack of competition allows the large banks to maintain much higher fees and thus higher earnings. One of the dirty little secrets of banking is that, as much as bank CEOs will publicly rail against the costs of compliance with regulation, in private they regard regulation as their friend, because regulation prevents competition.

The moat may alternatively take the form of a powerful brand, such as Coca Cola, in which Berkshire is also a large investor. Companies like to build strong brands because, again, having a strong brand allows a company to charge customers more than the product or service is really worth.

Berkshire Hathaway holds an annual shareholders' meeting in Omaha, Nebraska, where the company is headquartered, which is often referred to as "Woodstock for Capitalists", for the fervor with which shareholders flock to attend the meeting, to listen to the homespun wisdom of Buffett and Munger. The advice they receive is undoubtedly good, but as for the unofficial title of the event, it is a complete misnomer. Buffett, Munger, and Berkshire Hathaway are no more capitalists than any luminary of the left. Distorting capitalism through regulation and brand-building may well be good investment principles, but it acts solely in the interests of shareholders and company executives. It acts wholly against the interests of consumers, who would be much better served by the lower prices and better products and services which would be unleashed by competition and unfettered capitalism. One of the things which has been most damaging to the American economy is the misappropriation of the mantle of capitalism by actors who purport to be capitalists but who, in fact, subvert, capture, and neuter capitalism for their own selfish ends. The privatization of profits combined with the socialization of losses was a particularly corrosive outcome of the Global Financial crisis and promises to be so again resulting from the bank runs of early 2023 if the authorities do not handle the situation well.

In respect of the 2023 bank runs, the authorities should look to draw a careful balance. It is not efficient for each depositor individually to be expected to perform a credit assessment of the bank into which they plan to deposit their savings and the funds needed to maintain their checking account; nor should all depositors be expected to have the skills to perform such credit analysis. A deposit insurance scheme, such as offered by the FDIC, perhaps with an increased level of protection to, say $1m per depositor, is a sensible balance. Above that level, it is reasonable to treat the depositor as "sophisticated", and to require them to either buy their own insurance at market rates if they want further protection, or else to carry the risk of bank default themselves.

In recent years, the concept of "nudging" – the adoption of government policies intended to motivate particular behaviors – has become popular, especially since the publication of the book: *Nudge: Improving Decisions about Health, Wealth, and Happiness* by University of Chicago economist and Nobel Laureate Richard H. Thaler and Harvard Law School Professor Cass Sunstein. More recent research has indicated that the results of such nudging programs have fallen short of expectations, and, even when well-intentioned, have often led to unanticipated results. Knowing, as we do, that human societies are adaptive, we should not be in the least bit surprised by these observations, in particular that the adaptations people make are not necessarily those intended by the policy proponents. This begs the question of what business the government has in acting as the nanny state in trying to encourage us to adopt certain behaviors. Surely as adults, we can decide for ourselves which courses to follow and live with the consequences accordingly. Whilst we accept that the government, through taxpayers, needs to raise the money to fund the activities it undertakes on our behalf, and that in raising this money it should impose taxation in a way which minimizes economic distortions and certainly does not motivate adverse behaviors in citizens trying to minimize their exposure to the tax, nevertheless it is questionable whether government should impose taxes designed to discourage particular behavior which affect only that individual exhibiting the behavior (for example, taxes on sugary drinks), nor encourage, through the tax code, particular types of investments (for example, investments purported to exhibit certain favored environmental, social or governance (ESG) characteristics).

An example of nudging through the tax code is the incentive for people to buy the home in which they live, rather than rent shelter. Many countries have adopted tax policies particularly favorable towards residential real estate, with the best of intentions. Home ownership is one of the bedrock elements of the American Dream, after all. Home ownership is widely believed to be conducive to social stability; if people have a financial stake in the community in which they live, they are more likely to have an interest in seeing their community thrive and will take care to ensure it has lower crime rates and is less exposed to antisocial behavior such as littering and graffiti. Home ownership is more likely to encourage people to save the money they earn in order to save up for the down payment and then subsequently make their mortgage payments rather than fritter it away. For most people the home that they own becomes their largest financial asset.

However, whilst all of these aims are laudable, home ownership also has a number of downsides which are often little appreciated. For one thing, home ownership makes the labor force much less mobile and less able to move to where the work is as the economy develops over time. This is particularly a problem when there has been a downdraft in home prices after a long period of price stability or gently rising prices, because more recent purchasers of homes are often underwater on their mortgages and are unwilling to crystallize a loss by selling. It's also a problem after a steep increase in mortgage rates after a long period of low rates, such as we are experiencing in the U.S. at the time of writing in Spring 2023, because those people who have locked-in low mortgage rates in the past are reluctant to refinance a new home at the new, much higher, rates.

After a long period of rising nationwide home prices, as the U.S. had seen until the housing crash in 2007, people come to believe that investment in property is a sure-fire way to long-term wealth creation, which results in them overpaying to gain exposure to the market. To protect the value of their investment, property owners have increasingly voted in favor of highly restrictive planning laws, with the result that in popular parts of the country far too few houses are built to support a growing population, which further contributes to the inexorable rise in property prices, and further reinforces the view that investment in residential real estate is a one-way bet. But government-led distortions in the market lead to far higher prices than are justified economically for what should be regarded simply as essential shelter; a shortage of affordable homes for young people looking to start families and lives independent of their parents; and insufficient capital available to invest in the business innovations which drive productivity improvements and higher incomes.

A country's people cannot become wealthy simply by selling houses to one another at ever higher prices. This is simply wealth-illusion, as the wealth stored in real estate cannot be crystallized without selling one's home and not buying anywhere else to live. Whilst a handful of individuals may be lucky enough to sell their homes at inflated prices to foreign nationals looking for a place to invest capital, and then retire to live elsewhere where prices are cheaper, or rent for the latter part of their lives, such actions are not possible for the overwhelming majority of citizens who need or wish to continue living and working close to their current home, and collectively for U.S. citizens as a whole is impossible. The result is that a huge amount of capital is tied-up in residential real estate and is not therefore available to invest in business innovations which could increase productivity.

Zoning laws and the fact that local property taxes are used as the primary source of funding for the U.S. school system reinforces social divisions and increases class and wealth immobility, undermining another key bedrock of the American Dream; that, regardless of family wealth and background, anyone capable of hard work and diligent application can rise to the top.

What starts out as a well-intentioned sensible incentive from the government to engage in socially-desirable behavior – a family owning their own home – morphs over time into a grotesque economic distortion, undermining America's future. The road to hell is paved with good intentions. A more constructive U.S. government policy would be to simply get out of the way and let people make their own decisions.

CHAPTER SIX:

CENTRAL BANKS AND MONETARY POLICY

Central banks have been in existence for a long time and by now are regarded as a necessary component of an advanced economy, however it was not ever thus. The Bank of England, although only the world's eighth-oldest central bank, is taken as the model upon which most modern central banks are based, and was established on July 27th 1694, originally as a private company, to act as a banker to the UK government and to raise money to fund the war effort against France, England's long-time foe.

The United States of America survived quite happily without a central bank until the creation of the Federal Reserve System following an act of Congress in 1913, with the goal of enhancing the stability of the American banking system. This followed a series of banking panics in the late nineteenth century, and in particular the Banking Panic of 1907 (also known as the Knickerbocker Crisis, after the failure of the Knickerbocker Trust) in which the New York Stock Exchange fell by almost 50% from its previous peak and there were numerous runs on banks and trust companies as investor confidence evaporated. The Panic was arrested only after the financier J.P. Morgan pledged large sums of his own money and convinced other New York bankers to do the same, to shore-up the banking system.

The poor performance of the U.S. economy during the 1970s and early 1980s led to a series of acts of Congress, including the Federal Reserve Reform Act of 1977; the Community Reinvestment Act of 1977; the Full Employment and Balanced Growth Act of 1978; and the Depository Institutions Deregulation and Monetary Control Act of 1980. Collectively, these established what is today perceived as the Fed's "dual mandate" to support maximum sustainable employment and price stability, alongside the bank's responsibility for stability of the banking system.

In 1989, the Reserve Bank of New Zealand was the first central bank of an industrialized country to be granted independence in setting monetary policy, following several years of poor inflation and economic performance in that country under the previous regime, whereby monetary policy was set by the finance minister. In 1993, the House of Commons Treasury Committee in the UK recommended that the Bank of England be given a similar remit, following Sterling's ignominious ejection from the European Union Exchange Rate Mechanism. Subsequently, several academic studies seemed to show a connection between central bank independence and improved price stability, the latter of which underpinned superior economic performance over time. The reason for believing that an independent central bank gives rise to better inflation performance stems from the fact that government ministers may have short-term political incentives to manipulate interest rates and the economic cycle to the longer-term detriment of the economy; best to take the lever of monetary policy out of their hands completely and give it to independent technocrats not subject to such short-term motivations. Consequently, in the last thirty years in all the major industrialized countries, it has become an article of faith that the central bank must have independent control of monetary policy.

Faith in central banks' ability to control inflation largely stems from the success of Federal Reserve Chairman Paul Volcker, appointed by President Jimmy Carter in August 1979 when the U.S. was suffering from an extended bout of stagflation – a pernicious combination of stagnant economic growth coupled with high inflation. Volcker raised short rates to almost 20% to tame inflation, which preceded a subsequent 40-year trend of declining inflation in the U.S. and all the major economies. However, I think that Volcker gets too much credit for this achievement. He was given assists from two important factors: one being that workers from China, India, and other southeast Asian countries were joining the global workforce from this time, as were increasing numbers of women. In addition, President Ronald Reagan in the U.S. (and likewise Prime Minister Margaret Thatcher in the UK) were busy drafting legislation to curb the power of the trade unions, following many years of industrial strife. The combination of these laws with increased labor competition succeeded in weakening the bargaining power of labor, which accrued a much smaller portion of corporate earnings thereafter, and also led to lower prices for goods and services, and lower inflation over time.

In fact, there have always been differing degrees of central bank independence. Perhaps paradoxically, because the European Union does not have unified fiscal policy, the European Central Bank has a great deal of independence, having inherited the mantle of the Deutsche Bundesbank. Whilst ostensibly the governors of the U.S. Federal Reserve Bank are individually independent, the institution collectively is much less so. The period of stagflation in the 1970s resulted primarily because U.S. presidents Lyndon Johnson and Richard Nixon leaned heavily on Fed Chairmen Arthur Burns and William Miller not to raise rates to curb inflation, as they were intending to, because the presidents' feared that to do so would slow the economy and damage their political prospects. And it is quite possible that part of the reason the Fed was slow to raise rates in 2021 as the first signs of inflation were stirring was because Fed Chair Jay Powell, whose first term was ending in the first year of incoming President Biden's presidency, felt that had the Fed raised rates more aggressively before Biden had nominated him for a second term, then Biden would have been more likely to nominate someone else as Fed Chair, instead of Powell.

But in any event, I question the logic of divorcing control of fiscal and monetary policies, since ideally these need to work together harmoniously. I also question the direction of causality between central bank independence and good inflation performance. Is it that good inflation performance was really the result of independent setting of monetary policy, or is it rather, as I suspect, that the good inflation performance of major economies over the last forty years was due to globalization and weak labor negotiating power, over which central banks had absolutely no control? The central banks might have been simply serendipitous beneficiaries of this good inflation performance, and enjoyed their independence because, per Henry Ford's mantra: *"If it ain't broke, don't fix it!"*

At the time of writing in Spring 2023, the central banks, led by the U.S. Federal Reserve, appear to have broken something. Whilst inflation in the U.S. appears to have peaked and is now falling, it is still well above the target of 2% that the Fed has set, and the most-aggressive series of rate increases the U.S. has seen, doubtless being driven in part by the Fed's tardiness in making the first increase, by which time the genie of inflation was well-and-truly out of the bottle, has led to a number of runs-on-the-bank in both the U.S. and elsewhere, notably with Silicon Valley Bank, Signature Bank, First Republic Bank, and Credit Suisse.

Fingers are being pointed in many directions as to the causes of the current banking crisis, including the Fed's tardiness in raising rates, the Fed's having lowered rates far too much and kept them too low for too long, allowing risks to build-up in the financial system. The Fed is now raising rates too quickly and too high a level, given inherent weaknesses in the economy, and at politicians' weakening of the bank regulations put in place after the Global Financial Crisis.

Central banks are perennially tardy in their monetary policy actions; sometimes they move rates too much, sometimes too little, but whichever it is, you can rely on the fact that whatever they do, it will be too late. And how could it be otherwise? Although many market participants assume that the Fed, with its army of economists and data scientists numbering some 20,000 employees, assume that the Fed is omniscient, having superior knowledge and forecasting powers, the reality is that the Fed is more like the Wizard of Oz: all-seeing and all-powerful in popular supposition, but in fact with no more knowledge and power than the man behind the curtain. The members of the Board of Governors of the Federal Reserve are just as clueless about the direction of the economy as the rest of us, and, given the complex, adaptive nature of the economy, this is a classic example of a situation where the wisdom-of-crowds approach would be much more effective than is a committee of the great-and-the-good when setting interest rates.

The approach to monetary policy taken by the Fed has been fundamentally misguided since at least the time of Fed Chair Alan Greenspan. It was Greenspan who instigated the practice of flooding the market with liquidity when the stock market collapsed by ~ 20% in October 1987. With the benefit of hindsight, we can see that there were several technical reasons for the collapse, not least of which was the concept of "portfolio insurance", whereby program trades of sales of stocks and stock Futures were triggered as new low price-thresholds were reached, resulting in cascading waves of sell orders as prices made new lows. Circuit breakers were subsequently installed to prevent such panic selling in future, but the Fed had established the practice which became known as the "Greenspan Put" (and subsequently the Bernanke Put and Yellen Put, as the practice was adopted by successive Fed Chairs) of flooding the market with liquidity whenever there were jitters in the stock market. This asymmetric practice, whereby the Fed would support stock market weakness, but did not lean into irrational exuberance on the upside (other than by jawboning), conditioned the Pavlovian response in which the market expected similar practice in the future. The insurance on the downside which the Fed conditioned market participants to expect led exactly to the type of moral hazard problem of which I wrote earlier. The use of low interest rates to cushion financial markets and the economy on the downside has become a drug to which they have subsequently become addicted. Little surprise then that they and the banking system should have suffered withdrawal symptoms after the Fed lost control of inflation and was forced into the most rapid series of rate increases since the Second World War in a belated attempt to stuff the inflation genie back into the bottle.

The artificially low interest rates engineered by the Fed and other central banks around the world have led to a disastrous misallocation of capital. The reasoning why this is the case was laid out by the leading Swedish economist of the late nineteenth and early twentieth century, Knut Wicksell, in his paper *Interest and Prices*, published in 1898, and more recently by the American economist Hyman Minsky in the 1970s. To understand this, it is necessary to review the role of interest rates and money creation in the economy.

Many people are mistakenly of the impression that money is created by the central bank or the government treasury, but the overwhelming volume of money in fact is created by private sector banks. It is true that during the period of quantitative easing and the increase in central bank reserves, the proportion of money created by the private sector did fall slightly but remained at around 95% of the money in circulation in the U.S. economy.

Historically, there have been three competing theories of how banks create money. The one which bankers would have you believe is that banks are simply intermediaries which gather deposits from savers and make these funds available to borrowers, thus performing the two classic roles of banks: maturity transformation, by taking short-term instantly-accessible sight deposits and transforming them into long-dated loans; and credit creation to fund such things as business development and home purchases. Bankers would have you believe this because it sounds like a noble and useful activity; unfortunately, it isn't true.

A second theory of banking is the fractional reserve theory, in which an initial sum of money, say $100, in an economy is deposited in a bank, which then is required to keep a fraction, say 10% of this sum as a reserve or provision against potential loss, and the remaining $90 it lends out. That loan is then re-deposited in another bank (either directly by the borrower, or by the person to whom the borrower gives it in exchange for an asset or other product or service purchased by the borrower). The process can then continue, with the second bank retaining 10%, or $9, of the deposit, and lending out the remaining $81 to a second borrower. That second borrower then (either directly or indirectly) deposits the $81 in a third bank, and the process continues. In this process we have the concept of the "money multiplier", being the reciprocal of the reserve requirement of 10%: thus, a money multiplier of X10 in this example, as the original $100 is multiplied by a factor of 10 to create a grand total of $1,000 worth of deposits as the process continues to its conclusion. Unfortunately, this explanation of money creation by banks is also incorrect, although it is still taught at some universities.

The real theory of how banks create money is the simplest, and in fact the oldest theory, in that a banking license grants to banks the right to simply create money as if by magic, by the process of people coming to the bank and asking for a loan. In granting the loan the bank is literally creating that loan out of thin air, recording it as an asset on its balance sheet. When the borrower deposits the loan (either directly or indirectly) in another bank (or even the same bank) that second bank records it on its balance sheet as a liability. Regardless of how many banks are involved in the process as loans are created and the sums deposited, by collapsing the daisy-chain we can see that in fact what has happened is that a bank has used the magic beans of a banking license to create money out of thin air, which is then recorded in the banking-system's balance sheet as a new loan on the asset side, offset by an equivalent deposit on the liability side.

When money is created in this way, it may be used to finance one of three things:

1. Investment in better infrastructure or a business venture, either to create a new business or to further expand an existing business's operations.
2. Collateralized investment in assets which already exist, such as mortgage lending against real estate or stock margin lending.
3. To fund current consumption.

In his Financial Instability Hypothesis developed in the 1970s, Hyman Minsky explained how the three stages of an economic cycle develop. In the first stage of what Minsky called *Hedge Finance*, during which the economy is expanding again after a previous recession, risk perception of both borrowers and lenders is high and businesses rely largely on their own internal funding sources. Their external borrowing is low, and businesses are able to borrow and invest that money in a venture which will generate sufficient cash flows to pay back both the interest on the loan and the full principal over time. As the economic cycle develops and memories of the previous recession recede into the past, levels of risk perception fall and companies now are able to borrow from external lenders easier. Minsky refers to this phase of the cycle as that of *Speculative Finance*, during which the venture in which the funds are invested is able to produce cash flows sufficient only to pay the interest on the loan, but the principal must be refinanced with a new loan when it reaches maturity. Rising interest rates and/or falling cash flows from the venture as the economic cycle matures inevitably turn Speculative Finance into what Minsky refers to as the *Ponzi Finance* stage of the cycle, in which the venture isn't able to generate sufficient cash flows even to pay all of the interest, and increased new lending must be sought to pay-off the old loans.

Minsky's three stages correspond to the three things which commercial bank lending may be used to fund. Only the first is a healthy and productive use of credit, and this corresponds to a healthy economy with a high Monetary Velocity (the rate at which money cycles through the economy). Creation of credit to fund asset purchases results only in asset price inflation, such as much of the developed world economy has experienced in the years since the Global Financial Crisis. This is an unhealthy and unproductive use of credit, and results only in an increase on paper in the wealth of those who already own assets, whether they be houses, stocks, or cryptocurrencies. Finally, creating credit to fund current consumption is clearly unsustainable except as a short term stop gap. At a time of great economic stress when many people were losing their jobs, such as was experienced during the Global Financial Crisis and in the early days of the pandemic, it may have been necessary for governments to help those in distress to get back on their feet to avoid permanent economic damage; but this could only ever be used as a very short-term emollient. Otherwise, borrowing to fund consumption results only in future potential consumption being brought-forward to today, at the expense of that consumption in the future.

Governments of the major industrialized countries find themselves today in the situation that they have run up huge debts to finance consumption, now in the past, accelerating the amount of debt during the Global Financial Crisis and again during the pandemic. Having issued this debt, they now have few means available to generate an income stream sufficient to service it. The figure shown below, courtesy of the Federal Reserve Bank of St. Louis FRED database, shows the level to which the U.S. government debt to GDP ratio has risen.

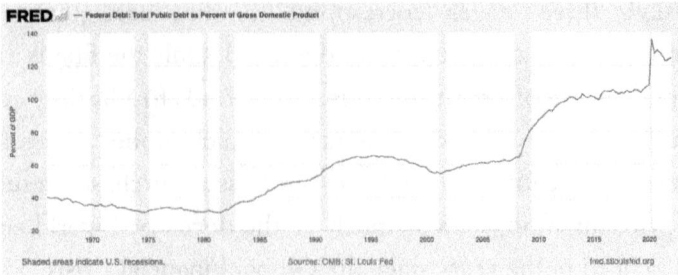

Far from politicians' belief that deficits don't matter, government debt must ultimately be repaid in one way or another, and until it is, it acts as a huge drag on economic growth, because the cash flow needed to service the debt must be diverted away from other, more productive, uses, causing monetary velocity to collapse.

Central banks' use of monetary policy (both conventional by adjusting short interest rates, and unconventional through asset purchases/sales and quantitative easing/tightening) to control the economy is predicated upon the so-called Equation of Exchange, an identity developed by the classical English economist and philosopher John Stuart Mill in his *Principles of Political Economy* published in 1848, expanding on an earlier idea of the Scottish Enlightenment philosopher David Hume. In its modern form, the equation was developed by the American economist Irving Fisher in 1911 and is expressed as:

$$\text{Nominal GDP} = P.Q = M.V$$

Where P is the price level, Q is an index of real expenditures on newly produced goods and services, M is the total average money supply in the economy and V is the monetary velocity, or the average frequency with which a unit of money is spent. Those with a background in physics or engineering may notice a similarity in the form of this equation with that from classical Newtonian mechanics for the momentum of a moving body:

$$\text{Momentum} = \text{Mass.Velocity}$$

with Nominal GDP playing the role of Momentum, Money Supply playing the role of Mass, and Monetary Velocity playing the role of Velocity.

Milton Friedman's espousal of monetarism as a means of controlling rampant inflation during the 1970s, and his view that "inflation is always and everywhere a monetary phenomenon" (in other words, that inflation is caused by too much money chasing a limited supply of goods and services) comes essentially from this equation. An increase in the money supply M will drive an increase of Nominal GDP, and if the increase in M is not matched by an increase in the amount of goods and services produced by the economy, then the increase in GDP will be manifested as an increase in the price level component (i.e., inflation), not an increase in real GDP. Friedman argued that to control inflation, it was necessary to control the money supply M.

It was for this reason that many economists expected the loose monetary policy achieved through interest rates being held at zero for an extended period, coupled with quantitative easing following the Global Financial Crisis, would lead to rampant inflation. However, their expectations were confounded as inflation remained benign, indeed below the target level of 2% for much of the time after 2008, until it started to take off in 2021. So why did inflation remain low despite the massive injection of central bank funds into the money supply?

The reason why Friedman believed that changes in the money supply led directly to changes in nominal GDP was that he believed that Monetary Velocity V was relatively constant, as indeed it had been for most of the time when he was active in research in the 1960s and 1970s. However, inspection of the data (see nearby figure, again courtesy of the Federal Reserve Bank of St. Louis FRED database), we can see that over the long-term V is highly variable. From being relatively stable at a level of ~1.75 from 1960 through the late 1980s, V then started to rise sharply and hit a peak of almost 2.2 around the time of the Asian Financial Crisis in 1997, whereupon it began a collapse which continued for the next 25 years, hitting a new all-time low of ~ 1.1 in 2020, below even the previous all-time low of 1.2 reached in the immediate aftermath of the Second World War in 1946.

So, as fast as the Fed was shoveling money into the economy after the Global Financial Crisis, the increase in government indebtedness was causing Monetary Velocity to collapse, offsetting the impact of the increased money supply on GDP and on inflation.

Velocity of Money 1900-2022
M2 V = GDP/M2
annual

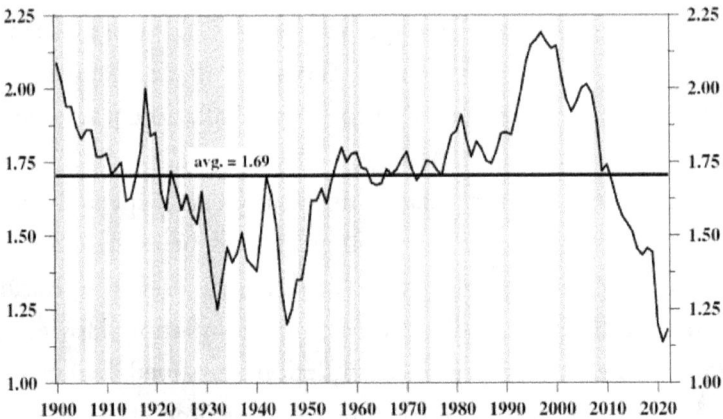

Sources: Federal Reserve Board; Bureau of Economic Analysis;
Bureau of the Census; The Amercian Business Cycle, Gordon, Balke and Romer. Through 2022.

In a strong economy where people spend money freely, money cycles quickly through the economy and Monetary Velocity is high, whereas low V occurs in a more sluggish economy with people holding onto money for longer and not being so willing to spend it. It's not surprising that V declined during the Crisis as people became fearful of losing their jobs, nor during the early days of the pandemic as a result of lockdowns and people staying at home, forcing them to hold on to their cash. But since then, as the vaccination program rolled out and people became more confident to go out to dine and to travel once more, Monetary Velocity appears to have bottomed and stabilized, albeit not yet increased markedly.

Empirically, V is also highly correlated with commercial banks' loan-to-deposit ratio. The causality of the relationship is that when debt is already at high levels a further increase in debt leads to an increase in the risk premium which a bank would need to charge as there is an increased likelihood of borrower default. The loan-to-deposit ratio declines when banks are unable to pass-on this increased loan cost to their potential borrowers, with the result that banks shift more of their deposits to funding pre-existing assets instead of making loans to businesses. In turn, bank investments in securities and other assets have a lower money-multiplier than do investments in loans to productive business ventures. Another factor driving the shift of bank lending away from business loans and towards purchases of government bonds was the change in bank regulations in the Dodd-Frank Act, to be discussed in more detail in the next chapter. It was a shift of this type which was the undoing of Silicon Valley Bank.

But to return now to our nineteenth century, Swedish economist, Knut Wicksell, identified two interest rates: the market rate of interest, being the rate at which lenders would lend, driven by the interest rate set by the central bank in a system with administered rates; and what he termed the "natural rate", a rate which is not directly observable, but which is driven by the natural return on invested capital, being a function of the rate of productivity of the economy. The difference between these two rates is referred to as the "Wicksellian spread", or "differential".

When the market rate is higher than the natural rate, entrepreneurs will not borrow because the marginal return on invested capital is below the level needed to service the debt. Such a rate structure serves to dampen economic growth and risks deflation and economic recession. When the market rate is a little below the natural rate, the return on investment is sufficient to service the debt and so entrepreneurs will borrow to invest. Initially the borrowing increases the money supply, but since the return from the investment is sufficient to service and then pay back the debt, the loan repayment reduces the money supply back to the original level. There is therefore no lasting impact of prices (i.e., no inflation) resulting from the temporary increase in money supply.

However, when the market rate is held artificially low by the central bank, as the Federal Reserve has done essentially since the Global Financial Crisis, it makes sense instead for financiers to borrow money at the artificially low rate, not to invest in new enterprises, but instead to acquire pre-existing assets. This corresponds to Minsky's *Speculative Finance* phase of the borrowing cycle, during which the financed asset is able to produce cash flows sufficient only to pay the interest on the loan, but the principal must be refinanced with a new loan when it reaches maturity. Subsequent rising interest rates and/or falling cash flows from the asset, as has been caused by the Fed's rapid series of interest rate increases since 2021, has inevitably turned the Speculative Finance phase into Minsky's *Ponzi Finance* stage, in which the financed asset doesn't generate sufficient cash flows to pay even the interest, and increased new lending must be sought to pay off the old loans.

Wicksell viewed the first form of borrowing: that by entrepreneurs to fund business investment, as a wholly positive increase in the capital stock. In contrast, Wicksell viewed the second form of borrowing: that by financiers to fund the acquisition of pre-existing assets, as wholly negative. Consequently, Wicksell argued that the authorities should aim to target the Wicksellian spread at a level close to zero, a target which central banks around the world have consistently ignored in recent years, most likely because they neither knew nor understood Wicksell's argument. In their ignorance, central banks have driven economies well into the realms of Minsky's Speculative and Ponzi phases, with disastrous results.

The best that may be said about central banks' policies of ultra-low interest rates and quantitative easing in response to the Global Financial Crisis and then the pandemic is that it seemed like a good idea at the time. It's impossible to know the counterfactual – what would have happened had the central banks pursued a different policy – but in hindsight (Wicksell and Minsky would say with foresight) these policies have been very damaging, causing speculative bubbles in asset prices, the bursting of which is leading to financial distress and bank runs, and further increases in wealth disparity, which in turn is leading to political damage to our democracy and our polity.

In their investigation of historical government indebtedness: *This Time Is Different: Eight Centuries of Financial Folly*, published by Carmen Reinhardt and Kenneth Rogoff in 2011, the authors show that when the government debt to GDP ratio exceeds about 90%, it usually leads to economic collapse. The ratio for the U.S. currently stands at a level around 127%, well in excess of the threshold, and the corresponding levels for other major economies are equally bad. Necessarily such excessive debt levels act as a drag on economic growth because the debt represents future potential growth brought forward, which now cannot happen again, and because the market knows that, one way or another, the debt will have to be repaid. All of the methods by which it might be repaid, either by much higher future taxation, or by default or repudiation, or by excessive inflation coupled with financial repression (i.e. forcing lenders to hold government debt whilst its value is destroyed by inflation, which was a technique employed by governments in the aftermath of the Second World War as a means of reducing the excessive debt built up to fund the war effort) are bad outcomes which will damage the reputation of governments as creditworthy borrowers.

Some ask whether debts may be expunged using the Debt Jubilees which happened in biblical times. Typically, those debts had been incurred by kings in pursuit of their war aims, and the money had been borrowed from a small number of wealthy nobles. Threatening the nobles with castration, evisceration, or beheading was usually sufficient to bring them to the negotiating table and forgive the debt. The problem today is that the debts have been incurred against a broad spectrum of citizens through our investment portfolios, pension schemes, IRAs, 401Ks, insurance policies, etc., and against foreign governments. In the end, as taxpayers, we owe this money to ourselves (or perhaps to our children and grandchildren), so debt forgiveness will not achieve much. The best solution would be to grow our way out of the problem by increasing GDP at a faster rate than the debt and interest payments thereon compound, but given that the debt serves to slow monetary velocity and acts as a drag on growth, this is much easier said than done.

I am left to conclude that central banks and governments collectively have done a truly terrible job of mismanaging the economy, as one would expect of a small self-anointed committee of the great-and-the-good in dealing with a complex adaptive system. Through its actions, inadvertently the Fed has driven all of the recent booms and busts in the economy, with all of the damage that these have wrought upon people's lives and businesses. The Fed's role largely consists of cleaning up the messes of its own creation. It would have been much better to rely on price signals and interest rates determined by the free market – the wisdom of crowds approach – rather than have rates be administered by an arm of government; in any event, the free market could hardly have done worse. Market-determined rates, as opposed to administered rates, would have been far closer to Wicksell's natural rate, leaving the economy far healthier and less prone to boom and bust. Note once more that my argument is not that prices and rates set by a free market are necessarily perfect, and maybe not even good – markets are subject to overshooting both on the upside and on the downside – my argument is simply that whilst free markets may be imperfect, they are infinitely better than anything else.

A further point is that whilst I have argued that having monetary policy set by a body of technocrats independent of fiscal policy set by the government does not make sense, it is not even clear that monetary policy is the best tool to manage inflation in the economy, despite the fact that this has become accepted wisdom. Consider that as a tool to manage inflation, monetary policy is actually quite remote from the thing we want to manage, being the combination of the money supply and monetary velocity, which drives inflation. Increasing interest rates to dampen economic growth, and so dampen inflation, works by increasing the price of money, which has lots of unintended consequences causing collateral damage to other parts of the economy, such as people looking to buy homes and to finance their businesses. Raising rates to dampen inflation is done with the deliberate intent to increase unemployment, the other half of the Fed's "dual mandate", and inflation also tends to harm the poorest in society the most. And whilst the Fed's actions in manipulating short rates certainly influence the economy, the idea that a $26 trillion economy can be *controlled* by the manipulation of short rates in the way that the Fed desires is frankly ludicrous.

A more direct way to control inflation might therefore be to adjust tax rates rather than interest rates, because taxation directly draws money out of the economy, and in a way which would impact the poorest in society much less, because the poor tend to pay little, if any, tax. This is one of the elements of Modern Monetary Theory, which, whilst having little else to commend it, is nevertheless correct in this regard.

An important question is where the 2% inflation target, now adopted by many of the world's major central banks, arises from in the first place. Why not a target of 0%?

In a capitalist economy, in the absence of changes in supply and demand, the natural state of affairs is for prices to fall, as competition encourages better and more efficient use of scarce inputs. Improved technology allows cheaper access to inputs too, for example, by opening up previously inaccessible raw materials such as tight oil and gas, through fracking. Overlaid on top of this long-term natural decline in prices are price changes due to changes in supply and demand. Changes in demand are driven by population increases and additional requirements for materials driven by new uses. Increases in supply may be driven by new technologies making additional, previously inaccessible, supply available, as well as declining demand from old uses, increased capability of recycling, and so on. It's often said that the cure for high prices is high prices (and likewise, the cure for low prices is low prices), because high prices will encourage more suppliers to come into the market to release supply they were unwilling to provide at the previous, lower price levels. So, in aggregate we have a classic complex adaptive system, with feedback loops between the various components of supply, demand, and long-term decline driven by competition and innovation. Despite the fact that the wisdom-of-crowds approach presented by a free market is infinitely better as a means of determining the appropriate price level, and the fairest means of allocating the scarce resource amongst the various participants, even to this day some governments will insist on instituting rationing and price controls to stop "rampant speculation" and other such nonsense. But in the absence of government and central bank interference, and aside from short-term temporary fluctuations, both up and down, caused by temporary fluctuations in supply and demand, the long-term trend in the prices of consumer goods and services would be down, and negative consumer price inflation would be completely harmless (in fact, a good thing, because it makes more things available to more people). This is what we observe in the prices of electronics, cars, clothing and other consumer goods: see the chart at the end of Chapter Seven.

While ostensibly central banks want inflation to remain low, they are wary of allowing it to fall too low and risk becoming negative, because of the deeply damaging effect that they fear negative inflation (i.e., deflation) would have on the economy. It's as though we want to take a walk along the edge of a cliff overlooking the ocean. The closer we can get to the edge the better our view will be, but if we get too close to the edge there is a risk that we might topple over and plunge to our deaths on the rocks below. So, we walk along the cliff a few feet away from the edge to lessen the risk of disaster. Central banks deem 2% to be an appropriately safe distance; in fact, the European Central Bank's target is framed as "below, but close to 2%".

The fear of allowing inflation to drop below zero – to become deflation – stems from the Great Depression of the 1930s, which saw mass unemployment and the failure of many farms and businesses and a cascading succession of bank failures. One of the great scholars of the Great Depression is Ben Bernanke, former Chairman of the Federal Reserve, and many financial market commentators took comfort from the fact that Bernanke was Fed Chair during the Global Financial Crisis, which is undoubtedly the biggest financial crisis the US has seen since the Great Depression. But the fact that someone has studied something deeply is no guarantee that they will come up with the right answer, and I am afraid that the fear that Bernanke and many mainstream economists have, of deflation in consumer prices, arising from the US experience in the Great Depression, is simply wrong. The error lies in the conflation of consumer price inflation with asset price inflation; in fact, these two are very different beasts.

Whilst consumer price deflation is entirely benign, the experience of the Great Depression was so bad because asset prices were falling (asset price deflation). Blown up in a huge speculative bubble based on cheap money during the Roaring Twenties, by the time of the stock market's Great Crash in October 1929 prices for all kinds of assets had inflated sharply. Much of the price increase was based on speculation as investors borrowed money to leverage their gains, and farmers borrowed against their land holdings to fund further investment. But leverage cuts two ways; when asset prices are on the way up it is great, amplifying positive returns, but on the way down it is disastrous, leading to a cascade of forced selling, which begets more forced selling. Asset price deflation is the thing which must be feared, but the best way to prevent asset price deflation is to prevent excessive asset price inflation in the first place, and the best way to prevent excessive asset price inflation is to avoid excessively cheap money (i.e., avoid having interest rates which are too low). But the Fed's actions since the Global Financial Crisis have been to keep interest rates very low, blowing up a speculative asset bubble in the prices of stocks, long-dated bonds, real estate, crypto, NFTs, meme-stocks and goodness knows what else. The Fed's actions of holding interest rates far too low in an attempt to prevent consumer price deflation, which would have been entirely benign, has been to inflate asset prices and risk subsequent massive asset price deflation – exactly the opposite of what it is trying to do. Truly, the Fed's incompetence is so spectacular that it would be funny were its consequences not so serious.

CHAPTER SEVEN:

CENTRAL BANKS AND BANK REGULATION

If we accept that the Global Financial Crisis and the political response to it were among the major drivers of political polarization and the increasingly negative views of liberal democracy and capitalism, the question becomes: what caused the Crisis? This question becomes of even greater importance given the series of bank runs in Spring 2023 leading to the collapse of Silicon Valley Bank, Signature Bank, Credit Suisse, First Republic Bank, and others, which occurred even after the supposed improvements in bank risk management and increased bank capital levels following the Dodd Frank regulation, the U.S. policymakers' response to the Crisis.

The Crisis and the bank runs were the direct result of policy failures leading to the buildup of risks in the financial system, the failure of banks to manage risks properly, and the failure of policymakers and supervisors to regulate financial institutions effectively. Poor policy making, poor regulation and supervision, and poor risk management led to systemic crises with dramatic effects. Although superficially a dry and arcane subject, bank regulation is of paramount importance: whilst you might not have much interest in bank regulation, do not think that bank regulation will have no impact on you.

In financial markets, risk is often defined in relation to the volatility of returns and conceptually is symmetrical in terms of both upside and downside market moves; but in the context of the impact on banking and financial market stability, it's more instructive to think about risk asymmetrically in terms purely of the potential for loss.

Experiments in behavioral psychology and what has become the field of behavioral economics have demonstrated that people do not behave in the way that theories of classical economics as applied to a purely rational Homo *economicus* assume. Probably as a result of survival behaviors learned on the African Savannah, human nature takes an asymmetrical view towards potential gains and losses; people abhor a loss much more than they take pleasure in making a gain of equal magnitude. This asymmetry explains why risky financial investments must earn a positive expected return in order to compensate the investor for assuming the risk of loss. This risk-driven positive expected return comes on top of a positive expected return even for risk-free investments, to compensate the investor for deferring gratification, another human trait which has been revealed by experiments in behavioral psychology. When an investor hands over money to another party, they are no longer able to use that money themselves until it is returned. Even when the party to whom the investor lends the money is guaranteed to return it on time (a so-called risk-free borrower, such as the U.S. government, because the investment bears no credit risk, although it may bear other kinds of risk), to persuade the investor to defer their ability to use the money themselves, the borrower must pay compensation to the lender in the form of an interest payment. The longer the period of deferral, the higher the interest rate used in the calculation of compensation must be, resulting in a positively sloped term-structure of interest rates, a so-called normal yield curve. The psychological phenomenon resulting in a positively sloped yield curve even for investments free of credit risk is referred to as liquidity-preference. The longer the tenure of the borrowing period, so the longer the period in which gratification from spending the money must be deferred, the higher must be the rate of interest used in the calculation of compensation for deferral. Interest rates are therefore often referred to as the time-value of money – the price which must be paid to persuade a lender to defer gratification. When the borrower is perceived as a risky-credit who may not pay back the borrowing on time or in full, a further compensation to the lender for bearing that credit risk is required, the so-called credit spread.

Credit risk and interest rate risk are just two of the many types of risk which banks take in the ordinary course of their business. From the bank's perspective, it's important to ensure that all of the risks, of all types, have been identified and the horizon must continually be scanned for newly emerging risks. Constant vigilance is required as the business environment evolves, because only when risks have been identified is there any hope that they can they be quantified, measured, monitored, and controlled to be within the organization's risk appetite, which is related, amongst other things, to the amount of capital it holds available to absorb losses and to its tolerance for earnings volatility.

Although banks have been in existence for several hundred years, when I left academia as a physicist at CERN, the European Center for Nuclear Physics Research in Switzerland, more than thirty years ago to join Wall Street and the City of London, risk management did not exist as a distinct and quantitative discipline. Of course, bankers, traders, and marketers would be held accountable by their employers for the quality of the deals they brought into the bank's portfolio, but risk management as practiced by banks and investment banks such as Goldman Sachs where I worked (still at the time a private partnership) was done wholly by the front office and the bank's managing partners. The Basel Committee of Banking Supervision (BCBS) had been set up in 1974, but it wasn't until 1988 that the Committee, under the Chairmanship of Peter Cooke of the Bank of England, first prescribed the minimum amount of capital which international banks should hold on the basis of their risk-weighted assets, with five categories of riskiness and a 100% risk-weight, yielding a requirement to hold a minimum of 8% of the asset value as capital; the so-called Cooke ratio, in what became known as the Basel Accord.

Sometime later, frustrated by the plethora of different metrics used to report disparate market risk-types, such as that of foreign exchange, interest rate Futures, government bonds, corporate bonds, equities, commodities,... held by the JP Morgan trading desks to the daily 4:15 p.m. Treasury Committee meeting which he chaired, Dennis Weatherstone, Chairman of JP Morgan, asked that a means be devised to aggregate these various risk-types into a single number. So was born Value-at-Risk, the classic statistical method to aggregate market risk, later adopted by the Basel Committee via the 1996 Amendment to the original Basel Accord, as a means by which sophisticated banks (those allowed to use their internal models) could calculate the amount of capital required to underpin market risk in their trading book, which generally produced a smaller capital requirement than did the standard model approach applied by supervisors to the less-sophisticated banks.

Since its first formulation, the Basel Accord has evolved considerably, as regulators sought to refine the approach in order to address criticism on both sides: on the one hand that the Basel capital prescription was too onerous and risk-insensitive, resulting in reduced lending to support economic growth; and on the other that it was too lenient and allowed the buildup of dangerous levels of risk which could threaten financial markets and the economy.

In response to these criticisms and through various market crises, in particular the Global Financial Crisis, quantitative approaches to risk measurement gradually became more codified and more prescriptive, and Risk Management became established as a distinct discipline. After a decade as a proprietary trader, I was at the forefront of what became a trend of having former-traders move to the independent risk oversight function (now known as the second line of defense, in contrast with the trading desk which forms the first line, Internal Audit which forms the third line, and the banking supervisors which form the fourth line) and contributed to the development of many of what are now standard techniques in the risk manager's toolbox, such as Value at Risk (VaR), Expected Shortfall (ES), Stress Testing, and Scenario Analysis.

Banks take many other types of risk as well as credit risk, supposedly captured via the Cooke ratio in the original Basel Accord and the trading book market captured via the 1996 amendment. In a reformulated version of the original accord known as Basel II, which came into force from January 2008, just in time to experience spectacular failure in the Global Financial Crisis, banks were also allowed to use internal models of default probability, loss given default and exposure at default for derivatives exposures in their statistical modeling of credit risk, replacing the standard risk weights of the Cooke ratio. For the first time banks were also required to hold capital to cover the catch-all "Operational Risk", defined as the risk of failed processes, people or systems. Again, the more sophisticated banks were allowed to use their own statistical "Advanced Model Approach" internal models to calculate their Operational Risk capital requirements.

However, as I have explained previously, like many frameworks which mediate interactions between people, financial markets are complex adaptive systems. As a reminder, complex adaptive systems are characterized by highly nonlinear behavior, which means that small changes in input parameters can have highly magnified impacts on outcomes. They have deep interconnections between different parts of the system, which means that the classic techniques of Stoic philosophers – of taking a complicated problem and breaking it down into its component parts; having experts solve each component according to their specialization; and then reconstitute the whole – do not work.

Also remember our earlier discussion about financial market behavior being much more akin to the world of quantum mechanics than it is to the world of classical physics. As a quick recap; in classical physics there is complete independence between the observer and the system under observation. Betting on a horse race, for example, is akin to classical physics, because of this independence. Whilst actions in the betting market change the odds for which horse is favored to win, they don't impact the outcome of the event, which is rather determined by the best horse on the day.

In the realm of quantum mechanics, however, the systems under observation are so small that the act of observation disturbs the system itself, described by Heisenberg's Uncertainty Principle. Betting in financial markets is like this world of quantum mechanics because in financial markets the actions of market players are not separate from market outcomes; rather it's the actions of the market players which **produce** the market outcomes, a process which George Soros refers to as "reflexivity". It's this interaction between financial markets and participants which results in markets being **adaptive**. Markets continually evolve over time and adapt to the actions of market players, including changes in market conditions imposed by supervisory bodies like the Federal Reserve and the Basel Committee.

This means that the use of historical time series data to estimate market risk (through Value-at-Risk and Expected Shortfall modeling) and credit risk (through Default Probability and Loss Given Default modeling) is problematic. Implicitly, when using these models, we assume that historical data are a good representation of the distribution from which future events will be drawn; but this assumption is justified only if the time series exhibit stationarity, or, in other words, if the statistical properties of the underlying processes generating the timeseries do not change. Since markets are adaptive, this assumption is not valid.

Given these concerns, consider the framework that the Basel Committee uses to determine the capital requirements for sophisticated banks under the Pillar I Risk Weighted Asset formulations. The Committee's approach is to perform separate calculations of capital required to underpin respectively credit-, market- and operational risks, and the results are then summed to produce the total capital requirement. But as I have explained, the interconnections between risk-types mean that such a separation is invalid, and the linear sum of the three components cannot be assumed to produce a prudent level of capital.

As an example of the interconnection between risk-types, consider the operational risk losses borne by banks and other financial market participants arising from the frauds conducted by Bernard Madoff. Madoff's frauds had been underway for a long time, and the suspicions of some participants had been aroused by the uncannily smooth financial performance of his funds; but what really brought the frauds into the open were the liquidity crisis and market risks arising from the Global Financial Crisis. It should not be surprising that risk of financial fraud may be heightened during stressful market environments, so clearly modeling operational and market risk capital requirements independently is inappropriate.

A forward-looking example of the link between market and credit risk might be the heightened risk of default of so-called zombie companies which have been kept on life support by the extremely low level of interest rates following the Global Financial Crisis and pandemic. As interest rates are now rising and economic conditions worsening, failing companies will be increasingly unlikely to be able to refinance their debt or grow their businesses, so are at increased risk of default. Moreover, the fact that interest rates have been so low for so long has enabled weak companies to continue to operate far longer than they would have been able to historically, a factor which is likely a driver of the lower productivity experienced in many economies. It is likely that such companies will have been run farther into the ground than would have been the case historically, so that Loss Given Default estimates (a key input into the calculation of the level of capital required to underpin a bank's credit risk exposures) based upon historical loss data may well prove to be too optimistic, and the credit risk capital so calculated prove to be insufficient.

Most of the time markets exhibit "normal" behavior and the inaccuracies induced by the invalidity of the assumptions are not too erroneous, but then most of the time a bank's expected losses are easily absorbed by its earnings from fees, commissions and trading bid-offer spread. The only times when a bank needs capital to absorb losses is during extremely stressful market periods when markets are moving with extreme volatility and counterparties and borrowers may be at heightened risk of default; but these are the very times when the assumptions underpinning the capital models break down most egregiously. Thus, truly are the regulatory capital models classic umbrellas which work only whilst the sun shines, yet the Basel Committee persists in using these flawed models.

The economist Frank Knight described the difference between "risk" and "uncertainty"; risk being the potential for adverse outcomes drawn from a distribution which is known, whilst uncertainty is the potential for adverse outcomes drawn from a distribution which is *not* known, the latter being what Nassim Nicholas Taleb refers to as "Black Swan" events.

In using historical observations to inform their view of potential adverse future outcomes, risk managers treat financial risks as "risks" (in a Knightian sense), in that they treat them as adverse events drawn from a known distribution. Risk managers do this because it is the only way to make risk quantification tractable. The truth, however, is that due to the complex and adaptive nature of markets, the future is fundamentally unknowable, and in reality, what risk managers are dealing with is uncertainty. Risk managers are like the man who is looking for his lost key under a streetlamp on a dark night. He is joined in the hunt by a friend, who, after some time of fruitless searching, asks, "Are you sure this is where you lost your key?" to which the man replies, "Oh no, I lost it over there!" "Well," his friend says, "if you know you lost it over there, then why are you looking here?" to which the man replies, "Because this is the only place I can see." "Risk Managers" call themselves thus and treat the uncertainties they are dealing with as risks because doing so gives them access to the only tools they have, and although they are not the right tools, they are better than nothing.

Whilst statistical metrics such as Value at Risk and Expected Shortfall are inappropriate for determining capital underpinning, they should nevertheless be a part of the risk manager's armory. For one thing, actual stress events are mercifully rare, and so although scenario analysis may be a better tool for determining minimum bank capital requirements, risk managers rarely get the opportunity to test those models. But if they use the same Profit & Loss representation (which tells how the value of a position changes with changes in the underlying market levels) and risk representation (which is used to express changes in the market risk factors feeding into the Profit & Loss representation) to calculate Value at Risk and Expected Shortfall as they use to perform scenario analysis, then the Value at Risk and Expected Shortfall metrics offer a relatively high-frequency measure of the adequacy of our Profit & Loss and risk representations through the daily performance of granular Profit & Loss predict-and-explain and granular back-testing.

The facts that markets are complex adaptive systems and that what risk managers are really dealing with is uncertainty, not risk, is why there can never be a silver bullet for risk quantification, and why, for all the developments in quantitative risk metrics and the formalization of risk management during the last thirty years, risk management will forever remain as much an art as it is a science.

Classically, there are two ways to aggregate disparate risk types; one is to model the behavior of a portfolio of risks statistically – create a distribution for each risk type, combine the distributions into one aggregate distribution and then look at the loss-tail of the aggregate statistical distribution at a sufficiently high quantile to measure the Unexpected Loss (Expected P&L is the mean value of the distribution). The other way is to look at the Expected Loss contingent upon a suitably plausible but adverse economic and market scenario – so-called scenario analysis.

Whilst the Basel Committee in its Pillar I rules focuses on statistical risk aggregation metrics, the Federal Reserve seems to have lost faith in statistical techniques (although the large U.S. banks under its purview are still subject to the Basel rules) and instead in its own domestic program has focused on scenario analysis, specifically in its Comprehensive Capital Analysis & Review (CCAR) program, applied to the largest U.S. banks. CCAR requires each bank to develop their own specific scenarios to which the bank would be exposed idiosyncratically, to complement the two general stress scenarios specified by the Fed – the Adverse Scenario and Severely Adverse Scenario, together with the Fed's baseline scenario.

In relation to Silicon Valley Bank, even if SVB had been subject to CCAR, the Fed's scenarios would not have highlighted the risks of SVB's business because the Fed's scenarios invariably involve a recessionary economic environment in which long-dated bond yields generally fall. SVB's portfolios would have shown profits in these scenarios through its positions in long-dated government and mortgage bonds. The Fed's scenarios did not include one in which interest rates rise sharply, causing a steep selloff in long-dated bonds. It was this exposure, coupled with the sudden disappearance of its deposits due to its bond portfolio losses, the fact that the deposits were largely uninsured, and the fact that social media allow bank runs to happen electronically and in very short timescales, which felled SVB. It's true that had SVB been subject to CCAR, the requirement for the bank's own management to devise scenarios which highlight its specific vulnerabilities would have been useful, but only if SVB's management had engaged in the process properly, which seems unlikely given their manifest failings in interest rate risk management and asset/liability management.

However, regulatory prescription of specific scenarios, such as the Fed does in the Adverse and Severely Adverse scenarios it specifies in its CCAR program, is extremely dangerous. The Fed applies these scenarios to all of what it regards as the largest, systemically important financial institutions, and requires banks to submit their exposures as well as the results of the application of the specified scenarios to each bank's exposures back to the Fed in very granular detail, in templates designed by the Fed. It does this so that it can aggregate the results across all of the largest banks and estimate the impact of the scenario across the industry (at least, across all of the largest banks, which cover the bulk of the industry's exposure). Clearly, such aggregate results are very useful to the Fed in helping to identify systemic risks, but the inadvertent consequence is to exacerbate systemic risk – exactly the opposite of what the Fed should want.

The reason is that the Fed's scenarios are all variations on a theme of what historically has been most damaging for banks: recessions in which the economy declines, unemployment rises, there is a steep selloff in the stock market, real estate prices decline, interest rates and bond yields decline, credit spreads widen, corporate defaults increase, financial market volatility increases, etc. Because banks want to minimize their exposure to such scenarios in order to reduce the amount of equity capital they are required to hold, which is driven by their losses in such scenarios, banks are motivated to reduce their exposures to precisely such scenarios. The act of modifying their business models to reduce their exposures causes the business models of different banks to become more closely aligned, thereby increasing systemic risk in the process. Some banks shed business lines wholesale as they are rendered uneconomic by the new capital rules banks are forced to adopt. As an example, consider the regulatory response to the Global Financial Crisis. Regulators identified that banks had held insufficient capital to underpin fixed income trading activity before the crisis, so they deliberately set about increasing Pillar I capital requirements for fixed income trading businesses in the temporary stopgap Basel 2.5 and then Basel III (and in what is, in all but name, Basel IV) versions of internationally agreed bank capital rules. The result was that one large bank after another shed much of their fixed income trading businesses, especially the European banks led by UBS, which had borne the brunt of the losses during the crisis, notwithstanding that the origins of the crisis were far from Europe, in the U.S. residential real estate market. Today, there is a much smaller group of banks which are active in the fixed income trading arena: JP Morgan Chase, Bank of America, Citigroup, Goldman Sachs, and just a few other smaller players. Under Bob Diamond's leadership, Barclays attempted to take advantage of the opportunity offered by the collapse of Lehman Brothers in buying the failed bank's U.S. business, but after he was pushed out due to the LIBOR fixing scandal, Barclays saw a retreat in fixed income, as did the other former European players such as Deutsche Bank and Credit Suisse. So, the consequence of well-intentioned regulatory actions was to concentrate most of the fixed income trading business within a much smaller number of Too Big to Fail banks, now each much bigger than they were before. Other fixed income trading activity migrated out of the regulated banks into the so-called shadow banking sector, consisting of hedge funds, private equity, and other unregulated financial institutions.

It seems there is an equivalent of the First Law of Thermodynamics operating with respect to risk in the financial system. The First Law is a statement of the law of conservation of energy with respect to thermodynamic systems: whilst energy may change its form, including the form of mass in light of Einstein's famous equation $E = MC^2$, it can neither be created nor destroyed. The same is true of risk; it may change its form and the way it manifests itself, but squeezing-out risk from the banking system does not destroy it; it is merely displaced to some other part of the financial system. It's an open question as to whether it would be better to keep the bulk of financial risk together, more transparently, in the banking system where supervisors could more easily keep their eyes on it, or whether it is better to fragment and disperse it wider, perhaps in the hope that by doing so it might cause less harm. In any event, by pushing risk out of the banking system, regulators may pat themselves on the back and be thankful that future blow ups may not happen in their bailiwick; but whether consumers and taxpayers will benefit from this remains to be seen.

Since the bank runs and failure of Silicon Valley Bank in Spring 2023, inevitably calls have been made to reintroduce the elements removed from Dodd Frank by the Trump Administration and otherwise to review the Fed's regulatory failings with a view to further strengthen bank regulation. Senator Elizabeth Warren has once more been on the warpath, claiming: "Banking should be boring. Banking is about making sure the money's there." Whilst it's true that when depositors visit the ATM to withdraw some cash, they expect the machine to deliver it, provided they have sufficient deposited funds in their account; but it demonstrates a fundamental misunderstanding of how banks work to suppose that if every depositor wanted to withdraw all the money in their accounts simultaneously, then they would be able to do so. The whole point of banks is their role in credit creation and maturity transformation, the latter being the taking of riskless sight deposits and transforming them into long-dated risky assets such as funding business innovations and mortgages for real estate acquisitions. Inherently, this process is risky, and it's the role of the bank's officers to assess the risks in the activities they undertake and to try to make sure they do it effectively and efficiently.

Already since Dodd Frank much risk-taking activity has moved out of banks and into the Shadow Banking sector. Thanks to the Volcker rule, banks are no longer allowed to do proprietary trading (except in U.S. government bonds – handy from the perspective of a government wanting to reduce its debt to GDP ratio by means of financial repression, or in other words, by forcing banks to hold government debt during a period of high inflation) and banks' investment in risky illiquid debt instruments have been rendered wholly uneconomic through onerous capital charges. The result has been that funding for innovative startup companies, the lifeblood of a dynamic capitalist economy, has been much harder for entrepreneurs to come by. Instead, banks now hold a much higher proportion of liquid government debt than they did pre-Crisis, the kind of positions which tend to profit in the types of CCAR stress scenarios run by the Fed to determine banks' capital requirements. Before the Crisis, around 80% of the largest U.S. banks' assets were loans, but today that figure has dropped to around 65%, with the difference having been taken up by U.S. Treasury bonds and government-backed mortgage bonds. So, the lesson learned from the Global Financial Crisis was that banks should reduce holdings of illiquid risky assets, which they then replaced with (supposedly) risk-free liquid government securities, and to rely much more on retail deposits instead of wholesale funding from the capital markets. The latter was because investment banks like Bear Stearns and Lehman Brothers, not being deposit collecting commercial banks, financed most of their inventory in the wholesale repo (securities repurchase) market with large commercial banks like JP Morgan Chase. It was JP Morgan's withdrawal from the repo market and refusal to continue to fund Lehman's positions (because of their concern about the true value of the positions Lehman wanted to fund) which caused Lehman's failure in 2008.

Now having seen Silicon Valley Bank blow-up as a result of holding exactly the preferred kinds of positions (i.e., lots of government bonds funded by large cash deposits), Senator Warren apparently now wants banks to hold only cash. It would, of course, be possible to eliminate risk-taking by banks, as Senator Warren apparently wishes, and force banks to hold a dollar of cash for each dollar they take in deposits, but then they wouldn't be banks – they'd be mattresses – and our economy would be much the poorer if they acted in that way. Notwithstanding Senator Warren's earlier proclamation: "I am a capitalist to my bones", such superficially well-intentioned but fundamentally wrong-headed political grandstanding will lead to total destruction of capitalism in our country.

Many observers of the banking sector in the European Union lament the fact that in Europe banking is so fragmented and that there are no EU-based global banking champions who can compete on a level playing field with the largest U.S. banks such as JP Morgan Chase. They would like to see cross-border consolidation of the industry within Europe to create more profitable EU-wide banks. Germany in particular is highlighted for its state-owned Landesbanks, which, with their favorable funding model outcompete the large private sector banks such as Deutsche Bank. But note that many of the most innovative and productive companies in the world are the small and medium-sized, often family-owned, businesses known as the Mittelstand. Thanks to these companies, Germany leads the ranking of the most innovative countries in the world, with more industry patents than any other. Such innovation requires a ready source of funding, and that exists in Germany largely thanks to the bank lending which that country's fragmented and highly competitive banking sector is able to offer. The United States is lucky in having extensive and deep capital markets available to finance its industry, and in the U.S., most funding of large companies is via the capital markets rather than by bank lending. But small companies, which are the lifeblood of innovation and employment generation in any economy, are too small to be able to access the capital markets and must rely instead on bank lending. (Note that large companies are more interested in automation and replacing employees with robots and artificial intelligence-driven processes to reduce costs and increase productivity, and in building anti-competitive moats to maximize profits without the need for innovation.)

In contrast, because the European Union is a union in name only insofar as its economy is concerned, it does not have deep, well developed capital markets, and so most industry funding in Europe is via bank lending. This is the reason why European governments, and the European Union, were unable to take a strong hand and force European banks to raise capital and clear out the bad loans on their balance sheets after the Global Financial Crisis in the same way that the U.S. did, in what became known as the Eurozone Crisis, or alternatively European Sovereign Debt Crisis, between around 2010 and 2015. Had they done so, it would have impaired the banks' ability to fund European industry, with disastrous effects on the European economy. But whilst the fragmented European banking industry with its small, highly competitive banks is less profitable than the U.S. banks, they are the reason why German industry is so innovative, highly productive, and profitable. Those who call for consolidation of the European banking sector to make it more profitable should be careful what they wish for; to do so might kill the goose which lays Germany's golden eggs.

And surely we should ask, what is the purpose of the banking industry anyway? Banking shouldn't exist as an end in itself; surely its whole purpose is to serve the real economy by gathering the savings of small savers and lending them, via credit creation and maturity transformation, to finance industrial innovations, boosting the economy, helping to create new jobs for workers, and providing a return for depositors. Elevating the status of banks to pole position in the economy, in the way that the United Kingdom has done, for example, has done a huge disservice to that country's real economy. Indeed, in many countries the financialization of the economy has been one of the banes of the twenty-first century.

Since the Global Financial Crisis was home-grown in the United States due to lax lending standards and a bubble in the residential real estate market, it's an interesting question as to how it caused so much damage to European banks. Perhaps we shouldn't be surprised to learn that this too was an inadvertent consequence of ill-thought-out regulation. The transmission mechanism which resulted in mortgages originating in the U.S. being transferred to European banks was as follows: U.S. banks have for a long time had a leverage ratio requirement which has controlled the quantity of assets, not weighted for risk, which banks have been allowed to have on their balance sheet. In contrast, in the period leading up to the crisis, the European banks had only a risk-weighted asset (RWA-based) capital requirement. Because return is generally proportional to risk, and mortgages were thought to be low-risk, the leverage ratio requirement in the U.S. motivated banks to securitize mortgages to get them off balance sheet, so they could free up their balance sheets for more-profitable activity. Not having a leverage ratio requirement, the European banks were happy to hoover-up the securitized U.S. mortgages because they were perceived to be low risk and therefore had a low RWA-based capital requirement. These different regulations in the U.S. versus Europe directly provided the transmission mechanism whereby several European banks blew themselves up as a result of exposure to U.S. mortgages, which in turn led to the European Sovereign Debt Crisis.

Minsky's description of the credit cycle which was discussed in the previous chapter explains why the smoothing-out of market volatility by the Fed's use of the Greenspan put led ultimately to the bubble which resulted in the Global Financial Crisis. In a capitalist, market-based economy, long periods of stability encourage excessive risk taking. Fair-Value accounting practices lead to higher collateral values during the boom period and thus allow ever more leverage. In this way, periods of stability beget booms which sow the seeds of future instability. As the bubble inflates, the fact that it is a bubble is rationalized-away by the invoking of new paradigms and new technologies which explain why "this time is different!"

An analogy with the Fed's actions to dampen stock market volatility has grown up within the financial community in relation to forest fires. In the past, the frequent occurrence of forest fires, although relatively small, led to a practice within the forestry service of immediately putting out all fires as soon as they started, before they could grow larger. But over time, this practice resulted in the building-up of large quantities of dry brush which would previously have been regularly burned and destroyed during the small regular fires. The consequence of this was that eventually so much dry brush tinder built up that the next time a fire broke out it quickly turned into a huge uncontrollable conflagration. The forestry service has now revised its practice and regularly undertakes small, controlled burning procedures to remove the brush before it can ever build up sufficiently to create a large fire. The Fed should take note.

But the problem of financial market complacency is the product of human nature and isn't confined to the participants and regulators of financial markets. A good example of regulatory complacency in a completely different area is that which led to the tremendous loss of life resulting from the sinking of the ocean liner Titanic on April 15, 1912.

As was the case in the Global Financial Crisis, the Titanic disaster resulted from a series of unfortunate events, accidents, bad decision making, and incompetence; but the most striking reason for the significant loss of life was simply regulatory failure. As is now well known, the Titanic had insufficient lifeboat capacity to enable all those on board to escape the doomed vessel. The reason it didn't have sufficient lifeboat capacity was that regulations didn't require it. The British Board of Trade, the body at the time responsible for maritime regulation, required that all vessels above 10,000 tons carry 16 lifeboats. The Titanic, at 46,328 tons, had 20 lifeboats, more than meeting the regulatory requirement. The reason that more lifeboats were not required was simply the result of regulatory complacency. At the time of the Titanic disaster, there hadn't been a major maritime accident in more than forty years and the Board of Trade regulations hadn't been updated in more than twenty years.

The thinking at the time was that the Titanic was unsinkable, and that lifeboats would be needed only to ferry people from a stricken ship to safety over a fairly lengthy period of time. It simply wasn't foreseen that the Titanic might sink so swiftly that there would be insufficient time for a ferrying operation to take place. Having the wrong mindset and a long period without incident fostered regulatory complacency, resulting in the regulations being followed unthinkingly. Regulatory frameworks tend to focus too heavily on fighting the last war, but the adaptive behavior of financial markets implies that future crises will unfold differently than previous ones, as, duly, we have seen in the way that the recent series of bank runs in the U.S. has unfolded.

In the aftermath of the Global Financial Crisis the regulations which the largest, systemically most-important banks are required to follow, have become so detailed and prescriptive, and so costly to implement, that the banks have effectively outsourced their thinking about risk management and capital requirements to the regulator, just as the directors of the White Star Line did for the Titanic. With highly specific, detailed, and expensive regulatory prescriptions, bank executives come to believe that not only is meeting the regulatory requirement necessary, but it is also sufficient. With this mentality, bank executives stop thinking about good risk management and instead risk management becomes little more than a regulatory compliance exercise. At one bank I know, which used to pride itself on its strong risk management, the CEO explicitly told their employees: *"We no longer seek to be best-in-class in risk management; all we seek is to be compliant with the regulations."*

Highly prescriptive regulations also create problems, because in motivating banks to manage their risks in a more-prescribed way, they cause banks to behave more alike, have more closely aligned and highly correlated positions, and more similar business models. As a result, they will respond to stressed market environments in a more-like manner. In this way, even as prescriptive regulation may make each bank idiosyncratically better risk-managed than it would have been without the prescription, nevertheless the effect of the prescription is to increase systemic risk.

An example is the requirement for banks to hold large quantities of liquid government bonds as a ready source of liquidity in a crisis, part of the Net Stable Funding Ratio and Liquidity Coverage Ratio requirements. Superficially, this sounds like a fine idea, but it only works if an individual bank idiosyncratically gets into financial distress. If there were a more-generalized market crisis, it's likely that liquidity, even on government paper, would completely dry up as many banks simultaneously tried to sell it. Liquidity is one of those quintessentially useless concepts; it's plentifully available when it's not needed but disappears immediately as soon as it is.

Unquestionably, banks required to adopt the Fed's CCAR and Basel Committee standards are each, idiosyncratically, better risk-managed and are much better capitalized than they were before the crisis. However, the assumption that if each bank individually is well risk-managed and capitalized, then the system as a whole will be safe, is false. Paradoxical as it may seem, rather than forcing a conformity of risk management practices upon banks, the better way to lower systemic risk would be to encourage greater diversity of risk management practices. And the observation that, through the inadvertent consequence of their actions, regulators bring about the very crisis they should fear the most would be funny were its consequences not so serious.

The importance of diversity, whether of risk management practices, or of an institution's staff composition, or the diversification of a portfolio of financial exposures, should not be underestimated. A good analogy for the importance of diversification is the experience of the Great Famine in Ireland of 1845–1849 when the potato crop failed over successive years, leading to more than 1 million deaths and a decline in the Irish population of nearly one quarter due to mortality and emigration. As is often the case in such disasters, there were several contributory factors, but one of the main drivers was the fact that a single crop, namely potatoes, was such a large part of the staple diet at the time and, worse still, the majority of growers were cultivating the exact same potato variety, called Lumper. Everyone was growing Lumper because of its high production of large nutritious potatoes; one can imagine the McKinsey of its day exhorting growers to grow this variety because it was market best practice! Adopting market best-practice sounds attractive, but it can lead to disaster if everyone does it. Just as genetic diversity enables biological systems to better withstand environmental shocks, and diversity of the staff members of an organization better enables the organization to be more agile and be better able to withstand disruptive changes to the business environment, so greater diversity of risk management practices would enable the banking system collectively to better withstand economic and financial shocks.

At the time of writing, in Spring 2023, shortly after the Silicon Valley and other bank runs, my criticisms of bank regulation may appear to be with the wisdom of hindsight, but this is untrue. As early as 2002 when employed by JP Morgan Chase, I gave a talk at the Bank for International Settlements in Basel, Switzerland, in which I highlighted the issue of prescribed stress scenarios inadvertently increasing systemic risk. It was as a result of this talk that I developed a friendship with Hyun Song Shin, now the Economic Adviser and Head of Research at the BIS.

And after the Crisis in July 2011, I was invited to give a speech at a Risk Management Symposium held at Cambridge University, hosted by the UK's Financial Services Authority (FSA), then the arm of the UK government charged with bank regulation after the Labour Government led by Tony Blair and Chancellor of the Exchequer Gordon Brown stripped these responsibilities from the Bank of England. Other than me, all of the speakers at this two-day conference, attended by senior executives representing banks operating in London, were from the FSA, explaining the UK's regulatory approach following the Global Financial Crisis. I was invited to give the final speech at the conference, entitled: "A View from the Banks – How Are They Changing Their Approach in the Wake of the Crisis?", in which I spoke of all of the points I have elucidated in this chapter. My speech was well received by the audience and afterwards the two senior FSA officials who had organized the symposium and invited me to speak said to me: "Paul, we agree with every word you said, although we would never dare to say so in front of our political masters!"

Likewise, I gave a similar speech in September 2013 entitled: "The Political and Regulatory Response to the Crisis: A Personal View" at the ETH Risk Day 2013, a Mini-Conference on Risk Management in Finance and Insurance organized by one of Switzerland's top business schools, the Swiss Federal Institute of Technology in Zurich, known as ETH-Zurich, and again at a Colloquium on Risk Management, Bank Regulation and Systemic Risk at Yale School of Management, attended by junior regulators from the world's major central banks as part of a course of study they undertake at Yale, and at numerous other risk management forums. I have a long track record of explaining why, for all that bank regulation is well intentioned, and the enhancements of regulation enacted after the Global Financial Crisis were intended to reduce the risk of future bank runs and a systemic banking crisis, the actions taken were poorly thought out and actually increased systemic risk.

Duly regulators' plan to prevent future bank runs failed to survive first contact with the enemy in Spring 2023 after the Fed raised rates aggressively over the previous 18-months in a belated attempt to regain control of inflation. Inevitably, the usual suspects blame the modest reversal of the Dodd-Frank regulations applied to medium-sized banks during 2018 and take the opportunity to demand yet more regulation. Albert Einstein supposedly said that the definition of insanity is to keep repeating the same actions in expectation of a different result. Far be it from me to question whether Senator Elizabeth Warren and her friends in Congress are *non compos mentis*, but we may be sure that any attempts to further strengthen bank regulation will have consequences no better than any of the previous attempts. Instead, we need a fundamental rethink of what society should want of its banks, and how better we might go about trying to achieve that.

It is not just in banks that we should rethink the need for, and the costs of regulation. Whilst a full discussion is beyond the scope of this book (I shall address these issues in a future work), I simply include the following chart showing the development of price changes for various goods and services, and of wages, between January 2000 and June 2022, courtesy of the American Enterprise Institute.

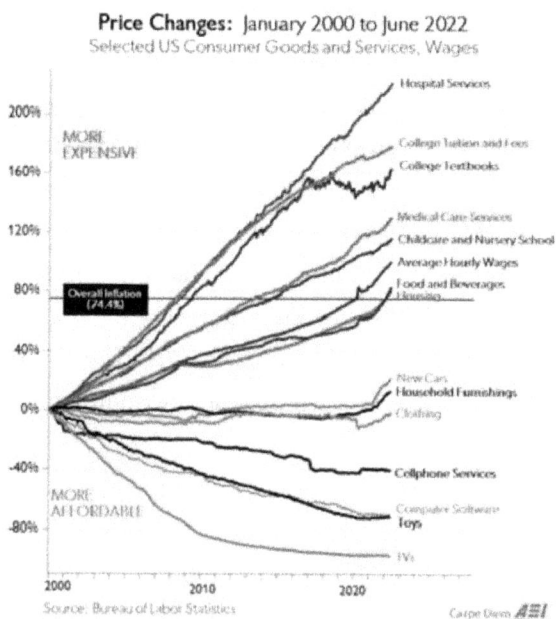

Price Changes: January 2000 to June 2022
Selected US Consumer Goods and Services, Wages

The chart shows that over this period, prices for many goods and services – TVs, computers, cell phone services, clothing, household furnishings, and cars – have fallen quite sharply, except for a pandemic-induced uptick over the last few years. On the other hand, the price of hospital and medical services, college tuition and textbooks, and childcare have risen sharply. What these latter goods and service items have in common is that they are all in highly regulated sectors, whereas the goods and services whose prices have fallen are all in unregulated industry sectors. This is the price we pay for regulation, whose dead hand removes competitive pressure and weakens incentives to improve performance, preventing the innovation and the use of technology which brings about the price reductions seen in unregulated industries, instead providing a moat which protects incumbents from competition and the Schumpeterian creative destruction which drives productivity increases and income gains for workers in unregulated sectors.

Government involvement in the highly regulated sectors of the economy, such as education and healthcare, also means that these sectors tend to have public policy goals, such as maximizing employment, which are not aligned with the interests of consumers and taxpayers, who would benefit from a primary focus on efficiency and increased productivity; in such cases, government acts directly against the goal of improving efficiency. This is exacerbated by the fact that the public sector remains heavily unionized, and whilst unions' role of protecting the interests of employees is legitimate, one of the downsides is that unions excel at resisting the job losses which drive productivity gains.

CHAPTER EIGHT:
A BETTER WAY FORWARD

The adaptive behavior of financial markets implies that the transmission mechanisms of monetary and fiscal policies will evolve constantly. Likewise, even without any evil intent or malice aforethought, players in financial markets, including banks and other financial institutions, will always try to optimize their behavior, given the constantly evolving set of opportunities and constraints governing their behavior; this is simply human nature. To expect a group of relatively poorly-paid and not-street-savvy bank regulators and supervisors – no matter how well-possessed they may be of academic qualifications – to police a group including some of the sharpest minds in the world, and whose financial compensation depends upon their ability to optimize the opportunity set (alternatively known as "game the system") is pure folly. Perverse as it may seem, the answer lies in *less* prescriptive regulation and instead in *more severe* consequences for the failure risk management by market participants.

Consider the situation when I first came to the City of London and Wall Street and joined Goldman Sachs as a junior trader in the Fixed Income division. At that time, risk management as a discipline did not exist, but Goldman was still a private partnership, as had been most of the Wall Street investment banks and city institutions until deregulation in the 1980s. The general partners of such a firm were exposed to the total extent of their net worth in the event that their partnership failed. Such exposure had the effect of concentrating the minds of partners wonderfully, and as a result they were well risk managed with little evidence of the unethical behavior which transpired in later years in such cases as the Libor and Foreign Exchange fixing scandals, and a great many Know-Your-Customer and Anti-Money-Laundering scandals. Of course, it would not be possible today to return to the days of private partnerships in banking as the amounts of capital required to underpin today's banking behemoths are far too large, but in considering the example of private partnerships, there is the germ of an idea which should be exploited.

Imagine if bank regulation today consisted simply of the instruction: you may do whatever you wish, but if your bank fails then the entire net worth of the bank's board of directors, C-suite executives and Managing Directors will be confiscated by the state and used to compensate taxpayers for whatever rescue has to be launched to bail out your failed institution. Such an instruction, I think, would concentrate minds wonderfully.

Before you object and say that no one would be willing to be a bank director or senior employee of a bank in these circumstances, consider that this was already the case in the days of the private partnerships like Goldman Sachs, so empirically we know that the objection is simply nonsense – the potential rewards of a Goldman partnership were always so great that people were prepared to take the risk of failure. And before you complain that such a requirement would result in bank executives demanding even higher levels of remuneration than they receive now in order to compensate them for the additional risk they are being forced to bear, consider that such a requirement be applied not just to banks but to the boards of directors and senior executives of all limited liability companies. The joint-stock limited liability company has been hugely beneficial in generating economic growth and allowing capitalism to flourish since it was first created by the Dutch government when it founded the Dutch East India Company (*Vereenigde Oost-Indische Compagnie* in Dutch, or simply VOC) in 1602 by issuing shares to the public in the world's first IPO. But the adaptive nature of financial markets means that even a mechanism which has worked well for more than 400 years may need to be tweaked occasionally, as it is not guaranteed to work well indefinitely due to market participants' seeking to game the system.

According to a survey of 350 of the largest U.S. companies by the Economic Policy Institute, realized CEO pay rose by 1,460% between 1978 and 2021, whereas the typical worker's pay rose by a mere 18% over the same period. The same survey shows that the ratio of pay of CEOs to workers rose from a factor of X20 in 1965 to a factor of X399 in 2021. At the time of the Great Panic in 1907, the banker JP Morgan argued that the maximum multiple of the average worker's compensation which a CEO should receive should be a factor of 20; he argued that beyond this a CEO was more likely to run the business for his own interest rather than for that of its shareholders.

And this growth of inequality has been one of several factors which has driven the idea many people have that the elite protected class is taking for itself a disproportionate share of the rewards of the capitalist economy, which in turn has been a driver of the growth in populism in recent years. In turn, these beliefs are driving the undermining of faith in capitalism as an economic model and in democracy as a political model. For their own good and to forestall the risk of the babies of democracy and capitalism being thrown out with the bathwater of inequality, it behooves the elite to address the issue of wealth inequality.

The feeling of grievance grows even more acute when the executives of failed banks such as Silicon Valley Bank are seen to have reaped considerable financial rewards in the years leading up to the failure of their institution, and then afterwards feel no remorse, are not subject to a claw-back of their egregious compensation and suffer no consequences worse than the loss of their jobs. Having been paid more during the period of their tenure than most people can dream of earning in a lifetime, even if they never work again, they can continue to enjoy a life of leisure and privilege. The fact that they did nothing illegal and so cannot be sent to prison does not soften the blow, and the fact that they too may have lost significant financial wealth as a result of the failure is irrelevant. It may be true that Dick Fuld lost $1 billion from his equity holding in the firm as a result of Lehman's failure; however, Dick had already extracted $1 billion from Lehman in the years leading up to the default. Losing half of his net worth as a result of stupidity but still walking away with $1 billion gives no satisfaction at all to the Joe Sixpacks and Jane Does who lost their livelihoods following Lehman's failure.

Penalizing shareholders for corporate failure or, indeed, malpractice committed by corporate executives, is also unsatisfactory, for we are all shareholders through our pension funds, annuities, and insurance policies, and it was always fanciful to suppose that shareholders might hold corporate executives to account. The key is not to punish external shareholders for corporate malfeasance or incompetence, but rather punish the corporate executives and board members who commit or oversee these acts.

To consider why this is the case it is instructive to review some aspects of the joint-stock company as market structures have evolved over time, and as a specific example to consider dual-class share structures.

The creation of limited liability equity as a funding mechanism proved to be extremely powerful in driving economic growth after its founding in seventeenth century Holland, and subsequently was adopted in Britain and elsewhere. Business founders are often in need of large amounts of capital to expand and grow their businesses by funding innovations which increase the business's productivity and profitability, generating surplus capital which can then be used to fund further innovations and productivity enhancements, in a positive feedback cycle, as well as pay dividends to shareholders. Likewise, investors who had savings were keen to put these to work to earn a return with which they could fund future consumption, such as pension investments to finance their lifestyle in retirement. Securitizing investment capital in the form of stocks and bonds enabled a much larger pool of investors to participate in the fruits of economic growth by sharing and diversifying risk, a wholly beneficial development.

Dual-class or multi-class capital structures, in which a company's founders and other privileged insiders retain a class of shares with high voting power, whilst the shares sold to the general public have a lesser voting power, have been around for a long time. Historically such structures were adopted by news media corporations such as The New York Times Company as a safe harbor to defend journalistic integrity and market independence, and by industrial titans such as Henry Ford at the Ford Motor Company. Like the Tech titans of today, the turn-of-the-last-century industrial titans had sufficient clout that an investing public who believed them to be geniuses were so desperate to invest their capital that they would accept the titans' demands that they provide investment capital but have little or no voting power. The rise in importance of the Tech sector companies in the early part of this century, with their iconoclastic leaders, has seen a burgeoning once more of the dual- and multi-class share structures (hereinafter referred to as dual-class share structures) as these companies came to market, led by Google (now Alphabet) in 2004. A recent Harvard Law School study claims that around 7% of Russell 3000 companies now have a dual-class share structure.

I'm sure the libertarians among us would argue that this is fine, and that if investors are so desperate to see a piece of the Tech action that they will accept second-class shareholder status, then what business does government or society have in interfering in a private contract willingly entered into by both parties? But I think that the divorce of voting ownership rights from economic ownership rights creates some serious issues which are the legitimate interest of society more broadly, and therefore of governments who should act to protect the interests of all citizens and taxpayers.

The problems of this divorce are exacerbated by the increased role of passive investing. Jack Bogle's key insight, that active asset managers could not, in aggregate, beat the market, and that because active investment is more expensive, after-fees the typical return to an investor in active funds is well below that of the market average, so investors would be much better off, on average, if they instead invested in low-cost passive investments, is incontrovertible. But the consequence of increased flows of capital into passive funds means that there is less and less effective shareholder oversight of company management.

Put the effects of passive investment and dual-class share structures together and you have a recipe for weak corporate governance and companies increasingly being run for the benefit of managers and corporate insiders rather than for their economic owners. One might suppose that it is the role of the board to exercise good corporate governance over the executive management team by acting on behalf of shareholders, but which shareholders? Those with economic interest, or those with the voting interest? Moreover, the typical CEO is hardly a shrinking violet. Company directors appointed to their boardroom seats by an imperious CEO, especially when the CEO is also chairman of the board, invariably know upon which side their bread is buttered. Any director attempting to reign-in a high-handed CEO's actions are likely to find themselves instead in ejector seats.

If neither board directors nor shareholders of corporations in which voting control is divorced from economic ownership can exercise effective governance over a company, then neither is market discipline since the economic ownership of the insiders of dual-class companies and companies owned through passive investment funds may, in principle, fall to very low levels without the insiders losing control of the company. Moreover, the voting rights of passive shareholders are often not exercised at all, and such shareholders don't even have the option of simply voting with their feet and selling their shares.

Historically, law courts have not regarded business judgment as being within their purview, leaving the oversight of management to shareholders and boards, which, in the normal course of events, are believed to have greater expertise. In the case of dual-class share structures, however, and increasingly as a result of passive share ownership, this leaves us with a situation in which there is no effective body exercising governance over managers, who have, in effect, been given a totally free hand and are under no obligation, as agents, to act in the best interests of the principals, being the economic owners of the company.

Some will look at the 420-year-old history of the joint-stock corporation and its success in driving economic growth and argue that it has stood the test of time and that we tinker with it at our peril. But as I have explained many times, markets are complex adaptive systems, and in any system possessing the property of adaptiveness, the fact that it might have worked well, even for centuries, is no guarantee that it will continue to work well indefinitely. As market participants come to understand its workings better, they may look to exploit aspects of the markets which were imperfectly understood previously – gaming the system. Eternal vigilance on the part of market participants and a market's supervisors is called for if the exploitation is not to become egregious. In the case of dual-class share structures, I think the exploitation in our capital markets has become egregious; it is high time to bring about the end of second-class citizenship. Moreover, as a result of the growing importance of passive investment vehicles, I believe that it is high time to review controls on the actions of management, and in particular of executive compensation.

Even though banks do not typically have dual-class share structures, they are highly leveraged and typically have only a thin sliver of equity underpinning a huge amount of risky assets, supplemented by an array of other liabilities of differing loss-bearing capacity, including deposits, straight debt, and (at least until the demise of Credit Suisse), large amounts of contingent convertible bonds, otherwise known as Alternative Tier 1 or AT1 capital. The consequence of this capital structure is that it is very difficult to instill market discipline upon the team of executives running a bank.

Bank executives frequently make the self-serving argument that banking needs to be a high-paying profession in order to attract the brightest and best candidates. But do we really want the brightest and best of our graduates each year to embark upon careers in banking when there are so many more useful and more fulfilling things that they could be doing with their lives and to benefit society? Of course, we want banks to be well-run; we want the payments system to operate efficiently; we want credit to be available to fund entrepreneurial activity and new business ventures; but we really don't need the cream of the output of our best universities and business schools to spend their lives inventing CDO-squared and other completely unnecessary opaque financial instruments. As former Fed Chairman Paul Volcker famously said: "The only thing useful banks have invented in twenty years is the ATM".

The bonus culture in the U.S., later copied in much of the world, stems from a research paper by academic economists Michael Jensen and William Meckling in the 1970s. Their insight was that the separation between ownership (which lay with shareholders) and control (which lay with management) created a lack of management accountability. Management, they felt, was liable to undertake empire-building or other activity which aggrandized the position of the CEO but did nothing for the welfare of shareholders. To address this principal-agent problem, they proposed that the CEO should be compensated largely in the form of equity or equity options in the company they managed so as to align the interests of company management with shareholders. Superficially, this argument is attractive, but it is simplistic as it takes no account of the personal financial circumstances, and therefore personal risk appetite, of each CEO, and the different abilities of corporate managers and institutional shareowners to diversify their respective risks. Moreover, performance related pay metrics are deeply flawed, with share price performance of an individual company being hard to discern from that of the overall market, and earnings-per-share metrics being easily manipulated through share buybacks at the expense of weakening the corporate balance sheet through increased leverage.

Consider also the Merton model, in which equity may be viewed as a call option on the assets of the company struck at the level of liabilities. Increasing the value of equity is therefore driven largely by increasing the volatility of the assets, and whilst this may be in the interests of external shareholders to some degree, as they have the capability to diversify risk in their investment portfolios, it is expressly not in the interests of consumers and contingent creditors of banks, in the form of the taxpayers who will be expected to pick up the tab for cleaning-up the mess in the case of bank failure. For this reason, bank executives should expressly be barred from owning any form of equity in the companies they serve, and instead should be compensated only with cash and deferred contingent convertible bonds.

Having stripped central banks of their responsibility for maintaining financial system stability because they have demonstrated their complete incompetence and inability to perform this task and thrust the responsibility instead firmly where it more-properly belongs, with bank executives and boards of directors, now let us turn our attention to responsibility for the management of monetary policy.

Just as central banks with their well-intentioned but fundamentally misguided regulatory practices inadvertently increase financial systemic risk, so with their flawed models of the economy do they inadvertently increase economic risk, being the direct cause of booms and busts through mistakes in administering monetary policy. Central banks should therefore be stripped of this responsibility, too, which instead should lie directly with financial markets.

Today, because we have grown used to the idea that central banks set the level of interest rates, we might think that their role in performing this task is essential, but this is simply not the case. Commercial lenders are perfectly capable of setting their own levels of the rates at which they are prepared to lend money, as are borrowers perfectly capable of deciding whether or not they wish to borrow at those rates. Rates set by the free market would be much closer to Wicksell's neutral rate, and as a result booms and busts would be far less likely. This is the way financial markets worked until governments started to interfere in the process. To be clear; I am not claiming that without interference from governments and central banks that financial markets are guaranteed to be problem free. Sentiment driven as they are, being the product of human interactions, markets are prone to overshoot and undershoot; from time-to-time banks will make poor lending decisions; sometimes borrowers will be too optimistic about the future prospects of their enterprises. But in attempting to correct what were perceived as the failings of unfettered markets, governments and central banks have made things infinitely worse and should simply be removed from the process.

The Alan Greenspan-led attempts to smooth-out volatility and remove booms and busts from financial markets have led to much larger, and much more damaging, (even if less-frequent) booms and busts, exactly as Minsky's Instability Hypothesis predicted they would. The role of setting interest rates should be returned to the free market. As was recommended by Walter Bagehot, son-in-law of the founder and onetime editor of *The Economist* in his book *Lombard Street: A Description of The Money Market*, published in 1873, the role of central banks should be limited thus: *"to avert panic, central banks should lend early and freely (i.e., without limit), to solvent firms, against good collateral, and at high rates"*.

CHAPTER NINE:

CONCLUSION

In this book, I argue the case that, despite the evident signs of human progress and business success all around us, the fact that human societies form complex adaptive systems underlies the observation that the future is fundamentally unknowable, and, as a result, decision making in the context of such a backdrop is fraught with difficulty and doomed to fail. That we can pick ourselves up, dust ourselves off, and start all over again is the saving grace of humanity. Recognizing that this is the case, we must organize ourselves in such a way that we are aligned with the grain of the fundamental problem, not try to cut across or go against the grain. Liberal democracy as the least bad way to govern ourselves and capitalism as the least bad way to organize our economy, sharing a common underlying filtering mechanism with that of the creation of life on earth itself, are aligned with the grain of nature and lead to our smoothest course, however rocky it may appear to be at times.

Centrally planned economies and the industrial policies of democratic governments are doomed to fail. No one, no matter how brilliant, has the ability to successfully pick winners reliably, so when government-favored industries inevitably fail, having the full-bore capital backing of the state behind them means that the consequence of their failure is economically disastrous, destroying much of the capital base in the process. Meanwhile, those who made the bad decisions are rarely made to pay the penalty for their failure, instead moving insouciantly from one well-padded government role to the next.

Although perhaps unable to articulate their thinking in terms of the mathematics of complex adaptive systems, nevertheless several politicians have had an instinctive understanding of why democracy is to be preferred and why the scope of government should be limited. Think of Winston Churchill and his comment that "democracy is the worst possible form of government, apart from all those other forms which have been tried from time to time". Think of the Founding Fathers of the United States and their desire, borne of their experience of King George III, to limit and enumerate those powers which the federal government should have. Think of Margaret Thatcher and her desire to "roll-back the frontiers of the state"; or of Ronald Reagan and his comment that "The most terrifying words in the English language are: I'm from the government and I'm here to help." Being now aware of the language and mathematics of complex adaptive systems, we may arm ourselves with the foundational underpinning which supports their intuition.

In contrast to democracies, authoritarian governments are prone to make bad decisions no less frequently than do democratic governments, but without the reset button of periodic elections and an ability to throw the bums out (even if only to replace them with another set of bums), such bad decisions always lead to doubling-down on failing strategies, ever more repressive actions domestically and warmongering internationally.

No politician could ever admit publicly what I have explained in this book about why democracy is best. How could they? My thesis is that democracy is best precisely because political leadership is inevitably about making mistakes; admitting that would be kryptonite to any politician. Only an outsider can say what needs to be said; in this way my role is akin to that of Jester in the Courts of the Kings of old; the only one who dares speak truth unto power.

Recognizing that political leadership incurs the overwhelming likelihood of failure, as does the attempt to start a new business from scratch, the best mankind can do is to muddle through, preserving enough capital and resources to support the next generation, and the hope that it might do better.

FORTHCOMING:

WHAT AILS AMERICA?... AND HOW TO FIX IT

In his second book, Paul Shotton once more dons the bells and motley to dare to speak truth unto power. America's origins as an experiment in democracy led to the greatest, most powerful country on earth in just 150 years. Whilst imperfect, like anything crafted by men, the United States is still the greatest country on earth, and its ideals are still the most noble of any country. But whilst America continues to hold great promise, it has increasingly strayed from the path the Founding Fathers set it upon, making a number of unforced errors as a result of well-intentioned, but ultimately misguided, desires to address the inevitable shortcomings of its democratic experiment.

In his first book: *Doomed To Fail*, Dr. Shotton explained why the essential nature of human society is complex and adaptive, which results in decision-making – the essence of political leadership – being doomed to fail. In *What Ails America?*, Dr. Shotton addresses the most egregious failings of American society today; education, healthcare, housing, taxation, crony capitalism, our legal system, crime and punishment, lobbying and political funding, organized religion and gun control, and argues that dealing with these problems is becoming urgent. Our country is suffering from political gridlock and polarization plumbing depths unseen since the Civil War. Our economic growth and productivity are weak and declining. Government indebtedness has exploded to levels seen previously only in wartime. Health outcomes in the United States are worse than those in developed European and Asian countries, despite our much higher expenditures on healthcare; even the progress previous generations made in increasing longevity has now reversed thanks to deaths of despair. And China's leader Xi Jinping plans to take advantage of what he sees as America's terminal decline to supplant the U.S. as global hegemon and avenge China's century of humiliation.

America is blessed with enormous geographical advantages and a polity comprising the most dynamic and entrepreneurial people on earth, many of whom self-select to come to the United States to raise their families and make their mark upon the world. Despite our nation's problems, there is no finer country in which to live, and there is still time for America to act to protect our way of life; but we need to act now if we are to preserve Lincoln's great hope "that government of the people, by the people, for the people, shall not perish from the earth".

Pre-order Dr. Paul's much-anticipated second book by visiting www. PaulsInsights.com

ABOUT THE AUTHOR

Paul Shotton was born in the United Kingdom and educated at the University of Oxford where he became a physics PhD. Intending to embark on a career in academic research, he worked at the European Center for Nuclear Physics Research (CERN) in Geneva, Switzerland, until deciding to make a career switch to join Wall Street, in which he subsequently enjoyed more than 30 years of practice in financial market trading, risk analytics, and executive leadership. His current roles include that of fractional CEO of Tachyon Aerospace, an aerospace technology company, and that of chairman and CEO of White Diamond Risk Advisory, which advises CEOs, boards, and startup companies in the finance and technology sectors. Paul developed his knowledge of markets and honed his insights in high-level trading and risk management positions at financial institutions in major metropolitan hubs, first in fixed-income trading positions at Goldman Sachs and Deutsche Bank in London, and subsequently in New York as global head of market risk management at Lehman Brothers and deputy head of group risk control and methodology at UBS. Paul is a frequent publisher of articles on economics, corporate governance, and risk management. Since boyhood, he has been a passionate gardener, observing it to be a great complement to his professional activities, and finding the peace, solitude, and serenity of the outdoors to be the perfect environment for the stimulation of creative thought. He lives in Ridgefield, Connecticut, with his wife Lynda and their two dogs. They have two adult children.

www.ingramcontent.com/pod-product-compliance
Lightning Source LLC
Chambersburg PA
CBHW070800300326
41914CB00053B/756